Praise for
THE OFFICIAL SOCCER MOM
DEVOTIONAL

Attention all mothers of the ankle-biter battalion and eye-rolling hormonal group! Here is a devotional designed especially for you. Loaded with inspiring stores, tons of humor and practical tips, *The Official Soccer Mom Devotional* is required reading for today's busy mom.

Dr. Kevin Leman
Author of *Making Children Mind Without Losing Yours*

Lynne Thompson has hit the bulls-eye for those moms whose lives are lived in the fast lane of kids' extracurricular activities. She captures not only the humor but also the heartbreaks of being a mom—while showing how through it all we can stay tuned in to God. Perfect for any minivan mom to read on the go!

Barbara Curtis
Mother of 12 and author of *The Mommy Survival Guide*

Lynne Thompson (a.k.a. Soccer Mom Extraordinaire) writes words of wisdom for busy moms to help us create space, focus on the goal, and keep our hearts in play. Witty, applicable and heart-hitting, Thompson's book is a perfect devotional for the minivan mom who is overloaded and overtaxed.

Tricia Goyer
Author of *Generation NeXt Parenting*

When I first read Lynne's book I couldn't help but think of all of the opportunities missed as I rushed my children from one sports practice to another. The idea of creating a scavenger hunt to clean out our van never crossed my mind . . . but then again, neither did the dozens of other creative tips Lynne shares with her readers. A must-read for every mother with active children.

Patty LaRoche
Speaker, writer and mother of two Major League Baseball players

As an official soccer mom herself, Lynne Thompson writes with the wit and wisdom that can only come from experience. Take two parts Erma Bombeck and one part James Dobson and you get Lynne Thompson and *The Official Soccer Mom Devotional*. Get this book into the hands of harried moms everywhere!

Dave Meurer
Author of *Good Spousekeeping: A His and Hers Guide to Couplehood*

Stop the minivan! I want to get off! Soccer mom Lynne Thompson understands the crazy lives we moms face as taxi drivers, cheerleaders and all-around good sports. *The Official Soccer Mom Devotional* is the perfect pick-me-up anytime you need to be refreshed and refueled. You might even find yourself laughing out loud, like I did. Pull over and enjoy!

Michele Steinhauser
Founder of Club M.A.W. (Mothers and Wives)

The Official
SOCCER
MOM

DEVOTIONAL

A Book of 50 Brief and Inspiring Devotions

Lynne Thompson

Published by Regal
From Gospel Light
Ventura, California, U.S.A.
www.regalbooks.com
Printed in the U.S.A.

Library of Congress Cataloging-in-Publication Data
Thompson, Lynne.
  The official soccer mom devotional : a book of 50 brief and inspiring devotions / Lynne Thompson.
    p. cm.
  Includes bibliographical references.
  ISBN 978-0-8307-4583-8 (trade paper)
  1. Mothers—Prayers and devotions. I. Title.
  BV4847.T48 2008
  242'.6431—dc22

                                                                    2007034016

1 2 3 4 5 6 7 8 9 10 / 10 09 08

Rights for publishing this book outside the U.S.A. or in non-English languages are administered by Gospel Light Worldwide, an international not-for-profit ministry. For additional information, please visit www.glww.org, email info@glww.org, or write to Gospel Light Worldwide, 1957 Eastman Avenue, Ventura, CA 93003, U.S.A.

To
Pete, Cassie, David
for believing

CONTENTS

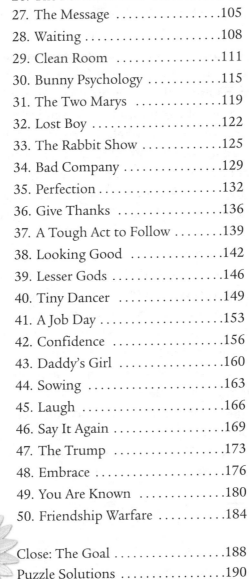

Acknowledgments

It's almost impossible to thank everyone who has helped me accomplish my dream; however, great appreciation goes to Daniel S. Robbins, my producer at Focus on the Family, who saw the potential for this project before anyone else. Special thanks to John Olson, who has spent a great deal of energy on this quirky writer. Much gratitude to Steven Lawson at Regal Books, who caught my vision right from the start. It has been a pleasure working with the Regal team—thank you for loving us soccer moms! Thanks to my agent, Steve Laube, a man of great integrity, who makes dreams a reality. A big thank-you to everyone at Focus on the Family for their ongoing support of my ministry.

I'd also like to thank:

Pearl Nelson, the mother everyone dreams of having.

Kathleen and Scott Prouty and the team of prayer warriors—you are the reason we hold this book in our hands.

Chuck Holton, for being a good friend, writing buddy and Christian brother, and to his sweet wife, Connie.

Amy Olson, travel agent and hospitable friend, who welcomed me to the Olsons' B&B.

My webmaster and dear friend, Kitty Robbins—you make me look good.

Gary and Mona Shriver, who support my radio ministry.

My online subscribers—thanks for traveling the journey with me.

Jon Drury and the Castro Valley team at Christian Writer's Seminar.

Marian Fritzemeier, John Vonhof, Pauline Youd and Chuck Roots, my gang at the Modesto Advanced Writer's Critique group.

My manuscript critique team: Audrey Rowe, Beth Swanberg, Dale Meurer, Pauline Youd, Dee Dawson, Jenni Long, John Vonhof, Don Rowe, Kelly Clawson, Julia Uselton, Tance Salafia and Michele Steinhauser.

Friends at Crossroads Church in Turlock, California, and First Baptist Church in Modesto, California, "Love the Edge."

Fellow writers who continue to support and inspire me: Dave Meurer, Chuck Holton, John Olson, Randy Ingermanson, Barbara Curtis, James Scott Bell, Tricia Goyer, Sally Stuart, David Kopp and Cecil Murphey.

The many staff, faculty and participants at Mount Hermon Christian Writer's Conference—I have learned so much from you.

Jeff Bradshaw from Jeff Bradshaw Photography for the author shots.

Soccer moms everywhere dedicated to getting their children where they need to be in this life and the next.

My family: Cassie, you are an amazing young woman whom I have the privilege to call daughter. David, you bring excitement and laughter into my otherwise routine life. I'm so proud of your tender heart. Pete, my best friend and the man of my dreams. You cooked and cleaned and didn't complain, not once. I love you.

And to my Lord, who heard my cry, lifted me out of the mire and set my feet on the Rock. Abba, this one is for You. May You receive the glory that is rightfully Yours.

FOREWORD

Are you having one of those days (or months) where you're feeling worn out, chewed up and spit out? If so, you're not alone. Millions of other "soccer moms" are right there with you—frazzled, frustrated and 100 percent exhausted.

Lynne Thompson feels your pain. She's a California mom, with two kids and a dog, who knows exactly what you're going through. This delightful little book comes right out of her personal experience as a wife, mother and semi-professional minivan driver. Like you, she's had days when she's been tempted to pack her bags, leave a to-do list for her husband and hop on a one-way flight to Maui.

Lynne speaks as a trusted friend—with honesty, vulnerability and a refreshing sense of humor. Her goal is to encourage you in your journey and point you toward the only One who can truly sustain you in times of emotional and spiritual drought.

As you read this book, I encourage you to meditate on the Scripture verses, pray the Mom Talk prayers and engage in the Mom's Space journaling exercises. If you do, I'm confident God will use Lynne's words to lead you to a deeper understanding of who He is and how much He loves you!

Dr. Bill Maier
Vice President, Psychologist in Residence
Focus on the Family
Colorado Springs, Colorado

INTRODUCTION

☑ Make breakfast and clean up.

☑ Drive tweenage daughter to church so that she can serve at Vacation Bible School.

☑ Go back home with 10-year-old son, pay bills and make picnic lunch.

☑ Pick daughter up from VBS, eat lunch on the church lawn and pick up four additional children for sports camp.

☑ Drive to neighboring town to drop off all children (except for daughter) at sports camp.

☑ Take daughter to orthodontist appointment.

☑ Drive daughter to pre-algebra class on other side of town.

☑ Go back to pick up daughter from pre-algebra class.

☑ Drive to nearby town to pick up the sports camp group.

☑ Meet friend at prearranged drop-off point to unload four sport-camp kids.

☑ Stop at a drive-thru for dinner.

☑ Drive to nearby town to pick up husband from work.

☑ Drop off daughter at church junior high group on the way to athletic club.

☑ Arrive at athletic club with husband and son for workout (elliptical, sit ups).

☑ Load everyone up and return to church to pick up daughter.

☑ Go home and collapse.

There are mothers across the nation who have a list equal to or more horrific than my own. We are the true road warriors, a sisterhood bound by our desire to make sure our children take advantage of the athletic, academic, musical, social and spiritual opportunities afforded to them. And that they get to these events on time!

Some call us "soccer moms," a tag given to mothers who spend enormous amounts of time transporting their progeny (and accompanying companions) to these various events. But we are more than that.

As Christian mothers, we are also passionate about their final destination. We pray that our little boys, with their over-active hormones and fearless risk-taking antics, grow up to become godly men who someday lead their families. That our little girls, with their quick words and dramatic responses, develop into virtuous women who someday nurture families of their own. We are the moms raising tomorrow's leaders.

Sometimes though, it's easy to lose perspective. In between the housekeeping, shopping and carpooling there are precious moments that, if not careful, we'll miss. Imparting life lessons: "Treat him the way you want to be treated." Expanding their world: "Let's do something new today." Stopping long enough to take in the beauty of nature around us: "Hey, let's get up to see the sunrise." Or the laughter—you don't want to miss the laughter.

Sometimes I lay awake at night reliving my day. I cringe when I think about the things I handled incorrectly or not at all. I become all too aware of my shortcomings and imperfections as a mother.

If you're like me, it's these times when it pays to remember that we don't have to do this parenting thing alone. God has promised to be there with us. Amidst all the chaos of motherhood, God visits us in subtle ways, like a sweet breath blowing into our souls, refreshing our spirits. Whispering to us, "It's going to be okay."

I've tried to slow down long enough to record a few of these gentle words. And because I know how busy you are, these stories are organized as short "mini-devotionals." I've also packed in a few helpful tools, interesting facts and some fun activities. Here is what you will find in each reading:

- *Soccer Momisms*—Some crazy things that moms often say

- *Mini-devotional reading*—"Mom stories" containing spiritual truths to encourage and inspire you

- *Mom Talk Questions*—A few questions to help you process what God might be saying to you personally

- *Soccer Mom Tips*—Tried and true solutions for moms on the go

- *Interesting facts, guides, quizzes, puzzles and more*—Short readings to help you pass the time while you wait for your child to finish his or her activity

- *Mom's Space*—Bible verses written in first person, with room for you to respond back in writing with questions, comments or gratitude after each verse, giving you a chance to Instant Message with God

So dig in and enjoy this break in your day. My hope is that you will be encouraged by this devotional and the profound (and oftentimes funny) ways God speaks to moms. Because no matter what the world calls us, our families will remember that with God's help . . . Mom got them there.

RUNNING AWAY

Have you ever wanted to run away from home?

It was one of those busy weeks: bills to pay, shopping lists to check off, church commitments to fulfill, dirty house to clean and a laundry pile the size of Mount Whitney, all combined with the duties of nurturing a rambunctious 10-year-old, a dramatic teenager, a husband and a pet rabbit. I needed a break—now!

I contemplated where to go. Hotel? Too expensive. Relatives? Too far away. The local coffee house? Not far enough.

I finally had to acknowledge that there was no place to go. I slumped down into the syrup-covered chair at the kitchen table: I was stuck right here at Soccer Mom Central. My Bible lay close at hand, right next to the cereal and milk that were left out. I began flipping through the pages, hoping for a revelation that would rescue me from my sorry state of mind.

In moments, I found myself sailing with Noah and his family, reveling in the way God keeps His promises. I flipped a few more pages and walked the barren desert with the children of Israel, humbled by the way God provides our basic needs. Then I jumped into the psalms and sat beside the quiet waters with King David, meditating on the goodness of God.

I got my wish that morning. I ran away into the Word of God. Upon my return, I was refreshed and ready to continue the rest of my day.

I'm not sure how, but these mini-vacations that I take into Scripture provide me with a much-needed break. I don't even have to worry about luggage or long lines at the airport. I'm planning another trip tomorrow. I've decided to travel with Job.

He *so* gets me.

!!! MOM TALK !!!

Is there a favorite book or verse in the Bible that helps you when you are overwhelmed? What biblical character do you most relate to and why? Pick a chapter in the Bible right now and plan a trip for tomorrow.

 Soccer Mom Tip
Before you begin your day, map out all your errands and try to organize them by location. This will cut down on time and gas expenses.

Bible Destinations

Location: Luke 5:1-11
Destination: Capernaum
Itinerary: Visit a quaint fishing village by the Sea of Galilee, home to apostles Peter, Andrew, James and John. Be amazed at the miraculous number of fish caught. Captain: Jesus of Nazareth.

Location: Exodus 14:15-22
Destination: Red Sea
Itinerary: Walk through the middle of a mighty sea, located
   along the western coast of Arabia. Enjoy supernatural views of
   a cloud pillar. Wind Advisory: Strong eastern winds predicted
   for most of the evening—dress accordingly.

Location: 1 Samuel 17:20-51
Destination: Valley of Elah
Itinerary: For the more adventurous, take a front-row seat on
   the battle lines near Judah and watch two adversaries fight to
   the finish. Beware of falling giant. Squeamish spectators may
   want to sit in the back.

Location: Daniel 3:1-30
Destination: Babylon
Itinerary: Visit the royal palace of King Nebuchadnezzar and
   his infamous 90-foot-high gold statue. Hear melodious tunes
   played on the horn, flute, zither, lyre, harp, pipes and other in-
   struments (we ask that you stand for all musical selections).
   Be amazed as three men, accompanied by one other, survive a
   blazing furnace. Idol melting to follow miracle.

Location: The Book of Ruth
Destination: Bethlehem
Itinerary: Romance is in the air as you travel from Moab to the
   barley fields of Bethlehem. Visit the town gate and lodge on an
   authentic threshing floor. Wedding to follow.

Location: Matthew 28:1-10
Destination: Golgotha
Itinerary: Visit the hillock above Jeremiah's Grotto, located in
   northern Jerusalem. Walk through the gardens, experience a
   mighty earthquake, see an angelic creature and be amazed to
   see a dead man raised to life! Beware of rolling stone.

Mom's Space

God: I am your rock, a fortress for you. I am your deliverer; you can take refuge in Me (see Psalm 18:2).

Mom:

God: This is your resting place when you are tired and weary (see Isaiah 28:12).

Mom:

Soccer Momism

"Don't make me stop this van!"

THE GRAVE

There is a tiny grave in my backyard that pays homage to a dead bird that was brutally attacked last spring. Its mound is covered with flower petals and a five-inch wooden headstone painted by my daughter. I hope to someday receive such an attractive burial. The event that caused the bird's demise, however, was anything but pretty.

My neighbor had come over to share a cup of tea as our children played outside. In a matter of minutes, the laughter turned to shrieks and my kitchen was soon teeming with sobbing children. Apparently a baby bird had fallen from its nest into our backyard, whereupon our dog, Molly, attacked the feathery intruder and killed it instantly. I tried to calm my six-year-old son, who was struggling with the reality of death.

"How could God allow this terrible thing to happen?" he said. "Doesn't He care?"

I knew how he felt. There are times in my life when I wonder if Anybody Up There notices *my* suffering, especially on days when I struggle with loneliness, or when the washing machine breaks down. But then I remember that God visited this less-than-perfect planet and offered Himself as the solution to our sin problem. He's walked in my shoes and shared in my human experience.

"Yes," I told my son, "God cares about the baby bird and about the death of everyone. But instead of walking away and leaving us alone, He came to visit us Himself. He lifts us up and places us back into *His* nest so that we can be kept safe under the wings of God."

!!! MOM TALK !!!

What are you suffering with right now? What are some of the ways Jesus may have experienced that same type of pain? Cry out to God with what concerns you most. He is ready to listen.

 Soccer Mom Tip
Make your used energy-drink bottles into quick on-the-go drinks. Refill them with water or fruit drink, then cap and store in the refrigerator until you head to the car.

Helping Your Child Process the Death of a Pet

- Allow your child time for asking questions and reminiscing about the pet.
- Provide a makeshift gravestone and burial site that your child can visit.
- If your child has a desire to express his or her grief, make art supplies available, such as clay, dough or paints.
- Create a scrapbook page highlighting the pet.
- Permit your child to keep an item that belonged to the pet, such as a pet tag, feeding bowl or doghouse.

Mom's Space

God: I will refresh you when you are weary and satisfy you when you feel faint (see Jeremiah 31:25).

Mom:

_____

_____

_____

_____

_____

_____

_____

_____

God: Cast your cares on Me and I will sustain you. I will never let the righteous fall (see Psalm 55:22).

Mom:

_____

_____

_____

_____

_____

_____

_____

_____

Soccer
Momism
"Of course I know where
I'm going."

MOCHA FAST

Have you ever experienced a mocha fast?

One of my dear friends was going through a tough time and asked for prayer. And even though I said I'd pray, I knew the truth. Too many times my "pray for you" promises didn't actually happen. I'd get sidetracked and then embarrassed when my friend later thanked me for my prayer support—which, I'm ashamed to admit, wasn't given.

But this time I was determined to remember. In order to stay faithful to my prayer commitment, I knew I would have to attach it to a daily activity. A habit, a basic need, a necessity . . . coffee! I made a decision to go on a mocha fast. Every time that I thought of making my way to the local drive-thru, I would instead pray for my friend.

A mocha-freak like me giving up coffee for a week meant that my friend was prayed for *a lot*. And because I told my friend about the decision, it helped this person realize the value I placed upon the prayer request.

When I made it to the end of the week, I celebrated with a grande double mocha. Strangely though, I found that it wasn't as enjoyable as it had once been. Apparently I'd substituted my caffeine addiction for another one—prayer. Make that a venti prayer . . . hold the whip cream.

!!! Mom Talk !!!

Who has God placed in your life to pray for? How can you remember to pray? Take a moment right now and bring this person's needs before the God who always hears.

 Soccer Mom Tip

For painting activities, try placing a soaking wet sponge in a tin pie plate as an alternative to an easily spilled cup of water.

Your Favorite Drinks

Rate your favorite drinks from 1 to 10:

_____ Coffee Misto / Café au lait

_____ Latte

_____ Mocha

_____ Espresso

_____ Hot chocolate

_____ Macchiato

_____ Tea

_____ Frappuccino

_____ Iced espresso

_____ Your favorite: _____

Mom's Space

God: Carry each other's burdens and in this way you will fulfill the law of Christ (see Galatians 6:2).

Mom:

_____

_____

_____

_____

_____

_____

_____

God: When you refresh others, you will be refreshed, too (see Proverbs 11:25).

Mom:

_____

_____

_____

_____

_____

_____

_____

Soccer
Momism
"You can do this. I believe
in you."

4

MONKEY ON YOUR HEAD

"Dinner's ready. Food's getting cold. There's a monkey sitting on your head."

It doesn't really matter what I say when my son's playing video games. My child's concentration level is so high, I'm sure half the house could burn down before he'd notice. There are times I'm irritated by his comatose stares at the glowing screen; other times I'm envious.

If only I could bring that level of concentration into my spiritual life. Mean words, bad thoughts, temptations and irrational fears would then merely be outside noise that interfere with my mission. The distractions that cause me to falter—such as a church squabble or someone else's bad attitude—would be seen as the intrusions they are, not deserving of my time or attention.

Instead, I can choose to look straight ahead, watching how God maneuvers me through the maze of life, teaching me how to overcome obstacles and empowering me with weapons to defeat the forces of evil.

I think I'll take a few lessons from my son. Then when life throws me a curve, I'll have my eyes fixed straight ahead on my Lord . . . even if there *is* a monkey on my head.

!!! MOM TALK !!!

Name a time when you had success in fighting a spiritual battle. What kinds of things are distracting you from your spiritual focus at this time? In Ephesians 6:11-17, Paul writes about putting on the full armor of God to stand against the devil's schemes. Which one of the following would help you right now?

- Belt of Truth
- Breastplate of Righteousness
- Shoes of Readiness and Peace
- Shield of Faith
- Helmet of Salvation
- Sword of the Spirit or Word of God

 Soccer Mom Tip
Have your child earn time to play electronic games by logging reading hours. Each minute earned reading to a parent can be redeemed for game time.

Soccer Mom Sudoku

The word "Sudoku" is derived from the Japanese phrase "*suji wa dokushin ni kagiru*," meaning "the numbers must be single" or "the numbers must occur only once." The basic objective of Sudoku is to fill a 9 x 9 grid so that each column, each row, and each of the nine 3 x 3 boxes contains the numbers 1 to 9 only one time each. On the following page are two original Sudoku puzzles of varying degrees of difficulty for you to complete. Good luck! (If you get stuck or just want to check your answers, the solution is printed on page 190.)

su | do | ku

© Puzzles by Pappocom
www.sudoku.com

2					3		4	7
4				5		8		
	6		7	4	9			
1		8		7		9		
	4	7	6		2	5	8	
		5		3		4		1
			3	9	7		6	
		4		6				8
3	1		8					5

VERY EASY   #1

			2		6			
		9				3		
	6	4				1	2	
9				2				7
			9		8			
7				4				5
	1	5				2	8	
		3				4		
			5		3			

MEDIUM

#2

Mom's Space

God: Submit yourself to Me; resist Satan and he will take off and leave you alone (see James 4:7).

Mom:

_____

_____

_____

_____

_____

_____

_____

_____

God: Fix your eyes on Me, the author and perfecter of your faith (see Hebrews 12:2).

Mom:

_____

_____

_____

_____

_____

_____

_____

A GREAT INVESTMENT

I tell my children that we are a wealthy family. Now, an economist might quickly point out most rich people don't drive a seven-year-old van, live in a small house or shop at bargain stores. He may mention that the elite—unlike us—dine out in fancy restaurants and hire a nanny, a chauffeur and a maid. This dollars-and-cents man might challenge my belief by dwelling on our overwhelming expenses and modest income, but he'd be missing the bottom line.

What we have can't be evaluated on a balance sheet. How do you project long-term benefits of a child who may someday save a life or serve a community? How can you estimate the value of an individual capable of riding out any calamity by holding fast to his or her faith? Today's financial wizards may not acknowledge the way we impart values like devotion and honest living, but someday business partners and spouses will appreciate our efforts.

Although our portfolio may not show it, we are a family fully invested in doing whatever it takes to raise responsible and godly human beings. And so far, our gain is very high. I guess you could say families are a great investment.

"The one principle that surrounds everything else is that of stewardship; that we are the managers of everything that God has given us."

Larry Burkett, Founder of Christian Financial Concepts

!!! Mom Talk !!!

What are some of the things you impart to your family that have eternal rewards? There are many ways God blesses families. Write down some of the ways God has met your family's needs. Take a moment right now to thank the Giver of all good things.

Soccer Mom Tip

Teach your children to share toys by setting a timer for a designated amount of time, allowing for each child to have a turn.

The Checkbook System for Kids

My children have their own checkbook ledgers to record allowances and expenses. It's convenient—the ledgers fit nicely between the pages of my checkbook, and I don't have to carry cash around. We balance the total at the end of each week, and everyone has a running amount of his or her spendable income.

Here are some tips on getting started:

- Extra ledgers and plastic cases are often available for free at your bank or credit union.
- Gift money from grandparents can be collected and deposited into the ledger.
- As an incentive to save, offer 2 "checkbook" dollars for every 10 dollars deposited into their savings account at the bank or credit union.
- A checkbook is a privilege that can be temporarily revoked if too many overdrafts occur.

- As children mature, deposit money for clothing and toiletries into their account and have them manage the purchases. They will be less apt to waste or wear out products.

Mom's Space

God: Remember: Your heart is in the same place as your treasure (see Matthew 6:21).

Mom:

_____
_____
_____
_____
_____
_____
_____

God: Don't be afraid; you are worth more than many sparrows (see Matthew 10:31).

Mom:

_____
_____
_____
_____
_____
_____

Matching

Shoe shopping isn't something you typically do with a 10-year-old boy, but I was desperate to find a white pair of sandals to show off my spring-season pedicure. I drove to Shoe Heaven— at least that's what my daughter and I call it—because it offers everything from stilettos to flip-flops.

As my daughter was holding up shoes for consideration, my son was preparing to hold up the store. At least that's how he looked with his face masked in women's fitting stockings.

I looked around, hoping that no one had noticed. They had, and their giggles were too loud to ignore. But since no one was reaching for her cell to make a 9-1-1 call, I returned to the task at hand.

"Look, Mom, don't these look like Amy?" my daughter called out, holding up a pair of lime-green pumps.

I smiled. She had inherited my gift for matching. For me, shopping is like connecting the dots. Any given item leads to a fond memory of a special person in my life. A rooster? Why that's my friend Julia. Birdhouses and teapots? That's my mom. Antiqued mirrors? It's Kathleen for sure.

I think one of the greatest joys of the human experience is to know someone and to be known. I love that God has made us all so different and that by noticing a person's particular tastes, we are recognizing their value as God's unique, one-of-a-kind creation. Of course, the best part is that God knows me, too: *Marquisate jewelry and mochas . . . oh, that's so Lynne.*

I finally gave up the hunt for shoes. I glanced back at my son, now darting around *Mission Impossible*-style. You know, I don't think I'll ever look at a pair of nylons without thinking of him.

!!! MOM TALK !!!

You're an original! In what ways do you stand out as God's special creation? What is your most favorite part of who God is? God has made only one you. Take time to thank Him for your custom-made design.

Soccer Mom Tip
Create your own trail mix and store in several sandwich bags, ready for your child to grab and go each morning before school.

The Shoe Quiz

What kind of shoes do you fill?

- ❏ Athletic shoes (I run everywhere!)

- ❏ Mules (No time to tie anything.)

- ❏ Heels (So I'm crazy, but I look great!)

- ❏ Flip-flops (I'm ready for land or sea.)

- ❏ Barefoot (Shoes? Who has time for shoes?)

Mom's Space

God: I created you in My own image (see Genesis 1:27).

Mom:

_____
_____
_____
_____
_____
_____
_____
_____
_____
_____
_____

God: I have searched you and I know you (see Psalm 139:1).

Mom:

_____
_____
_____
_____
_____
_____
_____
_____
_____
_____

Soccer
Momism

"Wow! Did you make that?"

LOVE'S HOLIDAY

This month I celebrated Valentine's Day, America's second-most lucrative holiday. When you find heart-shaped boxes of chocolate candy placed next to the half-off Christmas tree ornaments at the drug store, you know there's money involved! Each year my children invest great thought in deciding which package of trendy cards they need for their school party. Themes from baby animals and Ninja warriors to Scooby-Doo, the most important requirement is that nothing of any true affection is spoken in the written captions. A card proclaiming "Be mine" or "I love you" is pretty much dead in the water. The best cards are those that say nothing significant, but look really cool.

This shallow attempt at displaying fake affection was what motivated me to do something different this year. I decided to embrace the holiday by spreading love to everyone I saw that day. This meant that I didn't yell at the crazy person who pulled out in front of me in traffic, almost causing a three-car collision. I purposely smiled at the scowling, scruffy-bearded clerk who handed me my morning coffee, and I prayed for the man at the store who always asks to see my ID when I write a check, even though I've shopped at the same store for several years.

I waved to my nosy neighbor and stopped to talk with the postman. I joyfully volunteered to help out at church on Sunday.

Then I continued my love commitment by hugging the child who insisted his mother was evil when he didn't get his way. I laughed at all of my husband's jokes and told my teenager that she was practically an adult. I fed the pet extra that day.

As the day ended, I have to admit I felt very satisfied with my accomplishments. I loved unconditionally, and it felt very good. It almost made me wish I could celebrate all over again. I can hardly wait until next year.

!!! MOM TALK !!!

In what ways are you a challenging person? Who are the challenging people that God has placed in your life? What are some of the ways you can show love toward them?

Soccer Mom Tip
Date those precious works of art brought home from school and store them in a nice tapestry-covered box. Display the box in a prominent part of your home.

How Many Words Can You Create from

"VALENTINE'S DAY"

Example: NET

_____ _____

_____ _____

_____ _____

_____ _____

_____ _____

_____ _____

Mom's Space

God: I planned ahead and created good things for you to do for others. Do you know someone in need that you can help not only with words but also with actions (see Ephesians 2:10; 1 John 3:18)?

Mom:

_____

_____

_____

_____

_____

_____

_____

God: Shine your light so that others may see the good things you do and give thanks to Me, your Father in heaven (see Matthew 5:16).

Mom:

_____

_____

_____

_____

_____

_____

BEE-ING A MAN

The other day we picked up our vehicle from the auto repair shop, something that is becoming all too common. My daughter sat down in the passenger seat and screamed—there was a bee that had decided he deserved the privilege of riding shotgun. My daughter ran out of the vehicle and slammed the door behind her, trapping our insect passenger in the van.

Now I'm not positive, but I suspect God, in all His wisdom, has placed a switch inside of boys that instantly flicks on whenever a female shrieks in fear. I say this because my son, David, instantly turned into a commando warrior and headed directly toward the bee with book in hand. I tried to stop him.

"David, just open the door. The bee wants out."

No dice. Like the Terminator, he was programmed to destroy. David flung open the car door and thrust the book at his nemesis. And missed.

I managed to pull David from his intended hit long enough for the bee to escape. I was kind of frustrated with him, but then I remembered: God designed this plan before time began.

Our heavenly Father knew that woman would need a hero, and man would need someone to defend. He knew the bond between them could withstand any outside attack, physical or spiritual. Woman would cleave to man, and man would defend his beloved to the death. I saw the whole event acted out in a mini-drama before me, and it was quite satisfying.

Of course, the bee acted out his part too and fled for his life. He was no match for that kind of love.

!!! MOM TALK !!!

Who is your hero? What do you want in a hero that no person can fulfill? Take time to reflect on the superhuman qualities that only God possesses.

 Soccer Mom Tip
Have your child make up a new "code" each day for you to call when it's time to leave the park or clean up after playing. She will enjoy acting on the word "monkey" or "butterfly."

Word Bee

Fill in the missing letters on the right to make a synonym for each word on the left. (Answers are on page 190.)

1. disagree   o __ p o __ e
2. beginning   c __ m __ e n __ __ m e __ t
3. discipline   r __ s t r __ __ n t
4. harmony   a __ r e __ m e __ t
5. celebration   __ a r t __
6. children   o __ __ s __ r i n __
7. curious   __ n __ u i s __ t i __ e
8. sleepy   l e __ h a r __ i __
9. joy   __ l a __ i __ n
10. thankful   __ __ p __ e c __ a __ i __ e

Mom's Space

God: I know the plans I have for you. They are plans for your benefit not for your ruin. These plans will give you a future and a hope (see Jeremiah 29:11).

Mom:

_____

_____

_____

_____

_____

_____

_____

_____

God: I will comfort you in all of your pain so that you are able to comfort those in any type of pain with the comfort you receive from Me (see 2 Corinthians 1:4).

Mom:

_____

_____

_____

_____

_____

_____

_____

_____

Soccer
Momism
"Stop touching each other."

HEAVENLY TREASURE

My husband wanted his boys' Sunday School class to understand the dangers of storing up treasures on Earth instead of in heaven. So, unbeknownst to this group of 10-year-old boys, a little skit was carefully constructed. Pete met with our church youth director, and together they concocted a plan bordering on genius . . . or so they thought.

My inspired husband walked into class toting a sack of coins and started bragging about all the things he was planning on buying with the money. "First I'll get a video game, and then a remote control car, and then . . ." On and on it went until on cue, our youth director stomped into the class disguised in bank robber attire, snatched up my husband's moneybag and fled down the hallway.

Although this could have been the perfect object lesson about the temporality of earthly riches, things didn't quite turn out as planned. All 12 boys ran out of the room in hot pursuit of our poor youth director, took him down and retrieved the coins.

The message that day? Justice is definitely a heavenly treasure.

"Justice consists not in being neutral between right and wrong, but in finding out the right and upholding it, wherever found, against the wrong."
Theodore Roosevelt

!!! MOM TALK !!!

What are the injustices that bother you in life? Are they the same ones that bother God? Think of some ways God may want you to take action regarding these injustices; for example, writing a letter, making a phone call to your congressman or praying about something specifically. Thank God that He is just. Everyone will give an account someday to Him for all they do and don't do.

 Soccer Mom Tip

Avoid piles of clothes on the floor by setting up a family laundry center. Deposit dirty clothing into pre-marked laundry bags: whites, darks and colors.

Match the Currency with the Country

United States	yen
South Korea	won
Mexico	shekel
Japan	euro
India	shilling
Israel	peso
Italy	dollar
Niger	pound
Uganda	franc
Egypt	rupee

See answers on page 190.

 Mom's Space

God: I have shown you what I require of you—to act justly, to love mercy and to walk humbly with Me (see Micah 6:8).

Mom:

_____

_____

_____

_____

_____

_____

_____

_____

God: Defend the cause of the weak and fatherless; maintain the rights of the poor and oppressed. Rescue the weak and needy; deliver them out of the hand of the wicked (Psalm 82:3-4).

Mom:

_____

_____

_____

_____

_____

_____

_____

_____

_____

10

Soccer Momism

"We'll have to do fast-food tonight."

GOD KISSES

I call them God kisses: times in our lives when the God of the Universe uses a personal situation to say, "I know you." My time involved a broken-down van.

I was stranded in a parking lot with a dead battery and two children. *Great,* I thought. *Doesn't God know I have other things to do today?* So I called roadside service and waited. My children and I made the best of the time by picking wildflowers and enjoying a cool spring breeze. Finally, Roadside Assistance Guy came.

The monster yellow tow truck pulled into the lot, emitting clouds of exhaust everywhere. The man climbing down from the cab was husky and covered in oil. Just what this stranded customer ordered.

He graciously jump-started my vehicle, then delivered a lecture. Something about battery cables and corrosion, I think. He handed me the charge slip to sign on the back of a book, saying that somehow he'd lost his clipboard. Curiosity got the best of me, and I quickly turned the book over to read its title. It was *Anne of Green Gables,* by L. M. Montgomery. My favorite book.

I giggled, and he sheepishly said that it belonged to his child.

All I knew for sure was that I wasn't forgotten. God was right there giving me a kiss.

!!! MOM TALK !!!

What events have happened in your life that you believe were more than coincidences? What are some things about you that only God knows? Make a plan to spend a week looking for your "God Kisses," and write them down.

Soccer Mom Tip

Have your child call for a "job check" when finished with a chore or task to make sure it meets with your expectations.

Your Top-Five Favorite Classic Novels

My top-five favorite novels are: *Anne of Green Gables* by L. M. Montgomery, *Little Women* by Louisa May Alcott, *Pride and Prejudice* by Jane Austen, *To Kill a Mockingbird* by Harper Lee, and *An Echo in the Darkness* by Francine Rivers. List your top-five favorite novels below:

1. _____

2. _____

3. _____

4. _____

5. _____

List the last novel you actually finished:

_____

Mom's Space

God: If you, who are evil in nature, know how to give good gifts to your children, how much more can I, your Father who is in heaven, give what is good to you when you ask Me (see Matthew 7:11)?

Mom:

_____

_____

_____

_____

_____

_____

_____

God: I give to you, My love, even in your sleep (see Psalm 127:2).

Mom:

_____

_____

_____

_____

_____

_____

_____

Soccer
Momism
"Isn't that mine?"

11

LOST AND FOUND

It was time.

My son and I made our annual pilgrimage to the school's Lost and Found. I never lose that sense of wonder. The mountain before us could no doubt clothe a small country, maybe even two.

I don't know why they call it the Lost and *Found;* rarely have I seen anything reunited with its rightful owner. I've been told the majority of the items find their place at the local homeless shelter. And what a treasure they inherit: everything from Target specials to Hollister and Hilfiger. There are no class distinctions in a lost pile.

Perhaps our destination that day was really a microcosm of the world around us. Yes, many are lost and few are found, that's true . . . but what about those who already possess the treasure? Do we, like a distracted child, go off and ignore the priceless gift given to us? Do we throw it aside on the playground, not realizing the sacrifice the Father made to purchase the item?

I'm afraid I'm much too careless and laissez-faire with my gift. It was given at a high price, with great love and great cost. I'm concerned that one day I'll wake up and realize it's cold outside, the world is harsh and I've forgotten my jacket.

!!! Mom Talk !!!

What are some of the ways you show thanks to God for His loving sacrifice to you? What distracts you from your time alone with God? How can you build a daily quiet time with the Lord into your schedule?

> ### Soccer Mom Tip
> Light a candle every time your child starts practicing a musical instrument or reading a book, and then blow it out when he stops. Reward your child when the candle is melted.

Vehicle Scavenger Hunt

Clean up the car and rack up points at the same time!

Pen	5 points (20 points extra if it's chewed on)
Straw or a bead	5 points each
Money	5 points (20 points extra if it's sticky)
Used gum or a French-fry	10 points each
Ketchup packet	10 points (20 points extra if it's opened)
Hair scrunchie	5 points
Shoes	5 points for each one
Towel	5 points (20 points extra if it's wet)
Fast-food meal toy	5 points for each part
One mystery thing (nobody is sure what it is)	5 points
Homework paper	10 points
Candy wrapper	10 points
Receipt or scrap of paper with a phone number on it	5 points each
Sock	5 points (20 points if it smells bad)
Ball or used coffee cup	5 points each
A pizza coupon	5 points (20 points if it's expired)

Scoring
0 to 55 points: Give this book back to your wife.

60 to 110 points: If you're missing a child, look in the car first.

115 to 210+ points: You'd probably survive on a desert island as long as your vehicle went with you.

Mom's Space

God: I am standing at the door and knocking; if you hear My voice and open the door, we can visit together (see Revelation 3:20).

Mom:

God: Even though your sins are like scarlet, they will be as white as snow; though they are red like crimson, they will be like wool (see Isaiah 1:18).

Mom:

Soccer
Momism
"You did the right thing."

12

TRADING PLACES

My friend Amy and I joked about our godlike view at the gymnasium. The skywalk allowed us to peer down on our children playing in one room while our husbands engaged in a fierce game of racquetball in the next.

Then we heard screaming.

I looked down and saw my son lying on the floor, sobbing in pain. His foot had been caught in a beam, bending it almost completely in half. I was sure it was broken.

On the way to the emergency room, I elevated my son's foot and prayed. He looked at me through tears and cried, "I wish I were you right now so this wouldn't hurt."

My husband and I both responded that we wished the same—neither of us wanted to see our son in pain.

Our son was shocked.

"Why on earth would you want to be me?"

"Daddy and I love you," I explained. "We would trade places with you anytime to save you from pain."

And then a glimmer of understanding shone in the darkness, and I could almost hear my Father in heaven say, "And so I did."

!!! MOM TALK !!!

What sins from your past still haunt you today? You are unable to make things right yourself, so God laid down His life to take those sinful acts away. Write Him a thank-you note, acknowledging His sacrifice on the cross so that you no longer need to carry the guilt and shame.

Dear God

⚽ Soccer Mom Tip
Develop a family gesture that means "I love you" that can be related in public without words, such as scratching your chin or pulling on an ear lobe.

Mom's Space

God: I bore your sins in My body on the cross so that you might die to sin and live for what is right; by My wounds you have been healed (see 1 Peter 2:24).

Mom:

_____

_____

_____

_____

_____

_____

_____

_____

_____

God: I am the good shepherd, and the good shepherd lays down His life for the sheep (see John 10:11).

Mom:

_____

_____

_____

_____

_____

_____

_____

FISH TALE

My son and I dumped two bodies in the canal the other day. It all began with a birthday gift gone wrong.

My son had always desired a pet of his own. His sister had laid claim to Prince Charming, our Holland Lop Rabbit, and David had always felt left out when it came to animal ownership . . . but that all changed. Two weeks ago, he received two pet gold fish in celebration of his eleventh birthday.

Almost immediately, our entire family discovered that fish have issues. Who would have thought fish could expel smells that I'm sure are mentioned in the book of Revelation as part of the end-times plagues? No matter how many times we cleaned the tank, the stench remained. We needed to find them an alternative address, and soon.

We are not a cruel family, so the typical flushing down the toilet thing was out of the question. Especially since our daughter is a self-appointed enforcer for PETA. So David and I took a walk to the local canal. There the fish met their fate, and if PBS is correct, they are halfway to the ocean by now.

I dropped David off at school and left my husband a voicemail: "The package has been delivered." (The government is monitoring our calls now and you can't be too careful.)

The entire fiasco was quite enlightening for my son and me. He's done with pets, for now anyway. We both realized that most human beings don't really know what we want or what is best for us.

I'm so glad God knows me better than I know myself. The things I think are best, many times are not. My heavenly Father sees my future. He provides me with the things I truly need, and saves me from many bad decisions by telling me no. Otherwise, I too might be floating around in life, grasping for things that will never fulfill me.

!!! MOM TALK !!!

What things has God saved you from in the past by saying no? What are some of the things you think you need right now? Give those things over to God in prayer right now, asking Him to decide what is best.

Soccer Mom Tip

Put together a "Busy Box" of activities your child can do alone for those times you need to pay bills or return a phone call.

What Jesus Did with Fish

Matthew 17:27: "Take the first **fish** you catch; open its mouth and you will find a four-drachma coin. Take it and give it to them for my tax and yours."

John 21:6: "He said, 'Throw your net on the right side of the boat and you will find some.' When they did, they were unable to haul the net in because of the large number of **fish**."

John 21:9: "When they landed, they saw a fire of burning coals there with **fish** on it, and some bread."

John 6:11: "Jesus then took the loaves, gave thanks, and distributed to those who were seated as much as they wanted. He did the same with the **fish**."

Mom's Space

God: You do not know how to pray, but My Spirit intercedes for you with groanings too deep for your words (see Romans 8:26).

Mom:

_____

_____

_____

_____

_____

_____

God: I will meet all of your needs according to My glorious riches (see Philippians 4:19).

Mom:

_____

_____

_____

_____

_____

_____

SAY GOODNIGHT

It was 2:00 A.M. and the phone in the front room was ringing, which was rather strange—I don't keep a phone in that room. As I made my way through the darkness, I discovered that my child's play-phone had taken on a life of its own due to low batteries. At that moment, I did what any adult in a fog of semi-consciousness would do: I opened the front door and lobbed it onto the lawn.

Unfortunately, these kind of nocturnal disturbances are common. Parenthood brings with it so many joys; I guess it's only appropriate that in return, it takes a few things. Sleep is one of those things.

Now awake, I laid there listening to every sound that I usually sleep through during early hours: the refrigerator humming; the central air clicking on; the train a half-mile away; the familiar but ever-so-haunting creaking of an aging house.

Suddenly I heard a man's voice coming from my son's room! I jumped out of bed and ran down the hall, only to be greeted with, "I am Buzz Lightyear; I come in peace." *Well, isn't that reassuring.* The night ended with my son falling out of bed and my daughter joining me in mine, complaining of a bad dream.

This lack of sleep occasionally takes its toll on me. There have been times when I find myself driving and can't remember where

I'm going. Other times I frantically check the back seat, believing I've left one of my children behind.

Still, I wouldn't trade hours of sleep for the times I've been there to comfort a sick child or console a frightened heart. I know the night will come when I will long to once again soothe a fevered brow or kiss a soft chubby cheek, but they will have grown up and left. And I will be left dreaming of the nights when sleep was traded in for love.

!!! MOM TALK !!!

What are some of the ways you try to give yourself a renewal break each day (reading, napping, sitting down for a cup of coffee or tea)? It's important to take time to refresh. Plan your break for tomorrow. Sometimes taking a break with a friend is fun. Think about someone you can invite over or call on the phone.

 Soccer Mom Tip

Devise a family emergency plan with a meeting place locally and out of town. Memorize alternate phone numbers and emails for contacting each other if separated.

Cry Cures

Sometimes mothering can be overwhelming, especially when you have a fussy baby. Be proactive. Here is a list of ideas to try:

- Take the baby for a walk in the stroller or go on a short drive.

- Place the baby in a wind-up swing.

- Vacuum the house or play the radio. Babies sometimes love soothing noises, and it gives the caretaker a break from the crying.

- Relax. Lay the baby safely down in her crib and go take a warm bath.

- Ask a trusted friend if you could drop off your baby for a while.

- Put the baby in a safe place, like a crib or playpen, and leave the room for a while. Check on the baby every 1 to 15 minutes.

- Call for help. If you feel like you are going to lose control, do something about it. Contact your local church or Christian counselor. Some areas offer crisis support nurseries or women's support groups.

 # Mom's Space

God: Take My yoke upon you and learn from Me. I am gentle and humble in heart, and you will find rest for your soul (see Matthew 11:29).

Mom:

_____

_____

_____

_____

_____

_____

_____

_____

God: I will refresh the weary and satisfy the faint (see Jeremiah 31:25).

Mom:

_____

_____

_____

_____

_____

_____

_____

_____

No Big Deal

This past week I've been privileged to spend time with someone who holds an eternal perspective . . . my mom. I say that she has eternal perspective because nothing I deem a "parent 9-1-1" ruffles her at all. Messy rooms, childish tantrums and entire dinners hitting the floor are simply no big deal: My mom responds with that gentle Swedish smile and the words, "Years from now, this won't matter."

Deep down, I know she's right.

There are times I've sacrificed relationships over stuff that I'll probably donate to charity in a year or two. The emotional frustrations, though overwhelming at the time, will no doubt become the precious "I remember whens" of tomorrow. The accidents and mistakes of daily life may be embarrassing today, but they will soon become fodder for delightful laughter at future Thanksgiving Day celebrations.

Even today, I can think back fondly to the times that I got up for those 2 A.M. feedings, cleaned up messy toy boxes and rocked a restless child in my arms. Memory building is messy stuff. It's filled with tears and giggles, failures and triumphs. These events can build character or bitterness depending on how we handle them today.

As for me, I hope to be more like my mom. She's such a visionary.

!!! MOM TALK !!!

What are some of the things that went wrong last week? Do you think you will remember them a year from now? Think back to a month ago and try to remember something that you thought was huge but today seems pretty insignificant. Which of your own childhood stories or memories are the most precious to you?

 Soccer Mom Tip

Have your child work for his television time by riding an exercise bike or walking the treadmill while he watches.

Glory Days

Blast back to your past. What was a *big deal* in your day?

What we wore: _____

_____

Words or phrases popular at the time: _____

_____

Favorite songs: _____

_____

Favorite movies/TV shows: _____

_____

I remember when . . . _____

_____

Mom's Space

God: Consider it pure joy, whenever you face trials of many kinds, because you know that this testing of your faith develops perseverance (see James 1:2-3).

Mom:

_____

_____

_____

_____

_____

_____

_____

God: Give thanks in all circumstances, for this is My will for you (see 1 Thessalonians 5:18).

Mom:

_____

_____

_____

_____

_____

_____

_____

ROLY POLY

Tears rolled down my nine-year-old daughter's cheeks and onto her bug terrarium.

"He's dead!" she announced between sobs.

I held her close. "Roly poly bugs don't have a very long lifespan, honey."

"Will the bug be there in heaven, Mom?"

I confess that I do not hold any degrees in theology. But I defy any pastor that could prove to me from Scripture that roly polies are resurrected in the hereafter. Besides, that would mean that the spiders and snails would be there too . . . and the cockroaches. Imagine the cockroaches!

I told her that I didn't know. I did clarify that God created humans in His own image, not animals. I don't know if that really applied to our discussion about dead bugs, but it made me feel better.

She buried the insect in the backyard along with the dead bird and goldfish, and placed a fresh flower on top of the grave.

I prayed for her that night, realizing that my daughter's sorrow went far down into her heart, beyond my reach. I asked God to hold her and touch her in ways that I couldn't.

The next morning at church, I saw her cuddling the class hamster. She stroked him gently and then looked up at me with a big smile. Two minutes later she was petting Abby, the class dog. I realized God had answered my prayer. Some would call it pet therapy, but I call it God healing the broken-hearted.

It caused me to wonder if I just might see roly polies in heaven.

!!! MOM TALK !!!

What are you going through right now that no one but God can understand? Take time to give this situation over to Him, asking Him to handle it His way. Allow a healing time for yourself. Try visiting a pet store, working in the garden or browsing an antique bookstore.

 Soccer Mom Tip
Send encouraging notes tucked away in your child's lunchbox or backpack, or text message an "I luv u" to your child's cell phone.

Live Long and Prosper

EXTREME LIFESPANS OF VARIOUS ANIMALS

MAMMALS	YEARS
Beaver	19
Elephant	69
Chimpanzee	40
Grizzly	32
Hippopotamus	49
Horse	50
House Mouse	4
Mountain Lion	20

Squirrel	16
Tiger	25

BIRDS	**YEARS**
Canary	22
Eagle	55
English Sparrow	23
Great Horned Owl	68
Hummingbird	8
Parrot	80
Swan	102
Turkey Buzzard	118

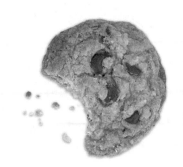

REPTILES	**YEARS**
Alligator	68
Box Turtle	123
Cobra	28
Giant Tortoise	152

AMPHIBIANS	**YEARS**
Giant Salamander	55
Green Frog	10
Newt	7
Toad	36

FISH	**YEARS**
Carp	47
Catfish	60
Eel	55

INSECTS	**YEARS**
Cicada	17
Ant (Queen)	15

Source: Forest Preserve District of Cook County (Illinois), "The Lifespan of Animals," Nature Bulletin No. 486-A, March 24, 1973. http://www.newton.dep.anl.gov/natbltn/400-499/nb486.htm.

Mom's Space

God: I will heal the brokenhearted and bind up their wounds (see Psalm 147:3).

Mom:

_____

_____

_____

_____

_____

_____

_____

_____

_____

God: Give your cares to Me and I will sustain you; I will never let the righteous fall (see Psalm 55:22).

Mom:

_____

_____

_____

_____

_____

_____

_____

_____

Soccer
Momism
*"Is your homework
done?"*

FIELD TRIP

The other day, I was Field Trip Mom. I visited the California state Capitol with my son's fifth-grade class. We traveled by school bus. You know: iPods, Gameboys, hand-clapping songs, windows needing to go up, windows needing to go down and students needing to sit down while the bus was moving.

Upon our arrival, I realized it had been three years since my last visit, yet I hadn't lost that sense of awe. Our capitol is quite impressive: sort of a miniature White House equipped with Corinthian columns, a dome and outdoor gardens. Although we didn't run into the governor, we had a nice visit with one of our California state senators. Of course the highlight for most of the students was chasing squirrels on the front lawn. My favorite part though was the Rotunda . . . or rather, what was in it.

On the first floor, directly under the dome, is a sculpture of *Columbus' Last Appeal to Queen Isabella*. As the title implies, it depicts Christopher Columbus appealing for funds from the Queen of Spain in order to set sail for the New World. He holds a sphere, convincing all that the world is indeed round, not flat. The words etched below read:

> *"I will assume the undertaking," she said, "for my own crown of Castile, and am ready to pawn my jewels to defray the expenses of it, if the funds in the treasury shall be found inadequate."*

Selling off your bling? Now there's a woman invested in a cause. Issa was definitely a big-picture gal. In her mind, present luxuries didn't compare to long-term benefits. So she laid it all down.

Gazing at the statue, I started to feel little in comparison to these two visionaries. My idea of sacrifice is to skip my manicure for a couple of weeks. As far as risk-taking, I sometimes order a double shot of espresso in my mocha. (*Whoa, look out!*) The statue made me begin seriously thinking about my cause. What is so important that I'd be willing to give up all of my worldly possessions to pursue it? What would drive me out of my comfort zone into uncharted waters? There's only one answer: God.

I began to assess how much sacrifice has thus far gone into my cause. What have I done with my riches or my time to further the message of God's hope to a fallen world? I want to take a serious look at my dedication and any missed opportunities. Because the last thing I want is for the Lord to return, only to find me chasing squirrels.

!!! MOM TALK !!!

What would take you out of your comfort zone? What opportunities might you be missing? Make a list of the causes you believe in.

 ### Soccer Mom Tip
Keep your mail in one basket for processing. Try to toss out unwanted junk-mail right away.

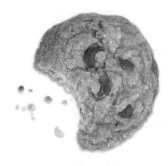

Capital Challenge!

List the capital for each state below:

Alabama _____	North Carolina _____
Alaska _____	North Dakota _____
Arizona _____	Ohio _____
Arkansas _____	Oklahoma _____
California _____	Oregon _____
Colorado _____	Pennsylvania _____
Connecticut _____	Rhode Island _____
Delaware _____	South Carolina _____
Florida _____	South Dakota _____
Georgia _____	Tennessee _____
Hawaii _____	Texas _____
Idaho _____	Utah _____
Illinois _____	Vermont _____
Indiana _____	Virginia _____
Iowa _____	Washington _____
Kansas _____	West Virginia _____
Kentucky _____	Wisconsin _____
Louisiana _____	Wyoming _____
Maine _____	
Maryland _____	
Massachusetts _____	
Michigan _____	
Minnesota _____	
Mississippi _____	
Missouri _____	
Montana _____	
Nebraska _____	
Nevada _____	
New Hampshire _____	
New Jersey _____	
New Mexico _____	
New York _____	

(Answers are on page 190.)

(Answers are on page 190.)

Mom's Space

God: Anyone who does not take his cross and follow Me is not worthy of Me (see Matthew 10:38).

Mom:

_____

_____

_____

_____

_____

_____

_____

_____

_____

_____

God: Make the most of your time, because the days are evil (see Ephesians 5:16).

Mom:

_____

_____

_____

_____

_____

_____

_____

_____

_____

_____

Soccer
Momism

"I need to meet her
parents."

THE DAY AFTER

I turn the calendar page and sigh. Another holiday come and gone. It never changes; I always experience some sense of disappointment the day after a holiday.

If it's the day after New Year's, I face the daunting task of undecorating the holiday tree. And no matter how creative I get, I will never be able to cram everything back into the storage box.

If it's the day after Valentine's, I'm transformed. Whereas yesterday I was the lovely princess receiving cards and flowers from my beloved, today I'm back to "pre-ball" Cinderella, donning sweats and scrubbing the sink.

If it's the day after Easter, I'm especially discouraged. I realize that sense of celebration I embraced during the church service pales in comparison to my everyday life. The glucose stares coming from my children who got acquainted with too many marshmallow chicks doesn't help either.

If it's the day after the fourth of July, I'm the janitor. Now, don't get me wrong, I'm thankful for our independence, but the streets littered with pieces of explosive debris make the Revolution look sanitary by comparison.

If it's the day after Thanksgiving, I've started my diet. A cruel yoke to place upon myself, considering that Turkey Day is only a precursor to the never-ending parade of winter treats delivered to my door or offered at company parties.

If it's the day after Christmas, I'm headed back to the mall. Apparently dear Aunt Suzie neglected to put much forethought into my gift. The last time I wore that size sweater I was having my braces removed.

There are many wonderful events to celebrate—graduation, marriage, birth of a child, a new job—yet no matter how wonderful the event, the next day will be . . . *less*. I think it's because deep down I know I was created for more than this world can offer. These celebrations are temporary, and my soul hungers for something longer lasting. Someday I will embrace an eternal existence called heaven, a place where all celebrations are ultimately fulfilling.

And the only thing better than that day will be the day after.

!!! MOM TALK !!!

What are your favorite holidays? What do you think holidays will be like in heaven? How might you celebrate today as a gift from God?

 Soccer Mom Tip

If you need to refresh but can't get away from the house, try a "lock-in." Have your husband or babysitter watch your child while you lock yourself in another room for two hours of uninterrupted you-time. Bring snacks.

Holiday Scramble

Unscramble the letters to find the holiday.

l t i n a n e s v e

_____ Day

t a r s i c m s h

_____

c t s r k t i s p a

_____ Day

s v p s e r a o

_____

n t h k g g s i v i n a

_____ Day

h j o y r f u t f l o u

_____

y o i r g a d d f o

_____

p i o l o s r a f l

_____ Day

b l r o a

_____ Day

m m i r l e o a

_____ Day

(Answers are on page 191.)

Mom's Space

God: Don't fix your eyes on what is seen, but on what is unseen. What you see is temporary, but what you can't see is eternal (see 2 Corinthians 4:18).

Mom:

_____

_____

_____

_____

_____

_____

_____

_____

God: No eye has seen, no ear has heard, no mind has conceived what I have prepared for those who love Me (see 1 Corinthians 2:9).

Mom:

_____

_____

_____

_____

_____

_____

_____

HARMONY

God has a sense of humor. I know He does. Why else would He allow a firstborn, task-driven, over-achieving woman to give birth to an easy-going, Type B, "chill out and smell the roses" child? Does He laugh when I huff and snort and shout demands that fall on apparently deaf ears? Does He giggle when my child neglects to turn in finished homework yet never forgets to send a thank-you card to those she loves?

I discovered at a young age that Cassie was marching to a different tune, one that didn't include a snare drum, but a violin. There are times when we try to change each other—I'm here to tell you this doesn't work—but we've discovered that we need each other.

I've been given a living, breathing example of the peaceful life. When I read in the psalms how King David was led by God to green pastures and quiet waters, I now know what that means (see Psalm 23:2). When God says, "Be still and know that I am God" (Psalm 46:10), I can picture what that looks like, thanks to my daughter.

Likewise, Cassie has a visual of the life that makes "the most of every opportunity, because the days are evil" (Ephesians 5:16). And she knows what hard work and dedication "as working for the Lord" (Colossians 3:23) is all about. Rather than berate each other for our differences, we have the opportunity to strive toward that wonderful balance the Lord desires for both of us.

She is my blessing and I am hers. I'm an eighth note and she is a rest. My desire is that instead of getting frustrated, we might make beautiful music together.

!!! Mom Talk !!!

What are some of the ways you and your child are different? In what ways do those traits become strengths in the hands of God? What strengths do you have that you can hand over to God for His use?

 Soccer Mom Tip

Get a giant play gate and place your toddler inside with tons of toys and a few snacks, then focus on your cleaning. Be sure to peek in on your little one every few minutes.

What Kind of Music Do You Like?

Rate your favorite in order:

_____ Classical

_____ Rap and/or Hip-hop

_____ Jazz

_____ Christian Contemporary

_____ Country

_____ Rhythm and Blues

_____ Classic Rock

_____ Hymns

Mom's Space

God: Live in harmony with one another. Be sympathetic, love as brothers and sisters, be compassionate and humble (see 1 Peter 3:8).

Mom:

_____

_____

_____

_____

_____

_____

_____

_____

God: If you walk in the light as I am in the light, you have fellowship with each other, and the blood of Jesus My Son purifies you from all sin (see 1 John 1:7).

Mom:

_____

_____

_____

_____

_____

_____

_____

Soccer
Momism
"That's not enough for breakfast . . ."

LEAP DAY

Every four years my son receives a birthday coupon from the ice cream shop in town. You see, the ice cream shop's computer doesn't recognize that we celebrate every year, in spite of his Leap Day birthday. The chance of being born on February 29 is about 684 in a million, so there are fewer than 5 million people who have their birthday on Leap Day.

For a while, my son was angry at the unfairness of being left out. Didn't they know about him? I assured him that even though the ice cream shop had ignored him, we wouldn't.

The same is true about God.

I'm so glad my Creator isn't like a giant computer that treats me like some code in a software program. My Lord knows I'm much more than a score on a credit report, a student identification number or another appointment at the doctor's office. I'm His child, uniquely created, made from a one-of-a-kind mold. He knows my needs, understands my desires and hears my prayers.

When I think of how big the world is and how many people occupy it, I'm amazed to know my God can keep track of us all. And I'll just bet He never misses anyone's birthday.

!!! Mom Talk !!!

When was the last time you felt like "just a number"? What are some of the things that are unique about you? Take time right now to thank God for singling you out as His beloved child.

 Soccer Mom Tip
On days when you feel stressed, occasionally misting your face with water can refresh and renew you.

How Unique Are You?

How common are the following recessive character traits? Check out the following percentages:

- 35 percent are born without wisdom teeth.

- 15 percent are left-handed.

- 30 percent cannot roll their tongue.

- 25 percent have attached earlobes.

- 25 percent place their right thumb over left when clasping their hands together.

- 25 percent do not have dimples.

- 25 percent do not have a widow's peak.

Source: "Teacher Guide: Comparing Inherited Human Traits," Genetic Science Learning Center, The University of Utah, 2002. http://learn.genetics.utah.edu/teachers/files/traits_comparing.pdf.

Mom's Space

God: Can a mother forget the baby at her breast and have no compassion on the child she has borne? Though she may forget, I will not forget you! (see Isaiah 49:15).

Mom:

_____

_____

_____

_____

_____

_____

_____

_____

God: Indeed, the very hairs of your head are all numbered. Don't be afraid; you are worth more than many sparrows (see Luke 12:7).

Mom:

_____

_____

_____

_____

_____

_____

_____

_____

Soccer
Momism

"Say you're sorry."

KNOW IT ALL

We have a strange saying in our home. Once a family member utters this motto, we all nod in understanding: "Spit a bug." I know, I warned you it was strange. It all began with a story I told my children during morning devotions.

Once there was a boy who rode his bike down the street. A little girl watched the boy from a distance when suddenly he turned his head and spit. "How disgusting!" the girl shrieked. She didn't want anything to do with a gross boy like that! Then the boy continued down the street, thankful he was able to spit that nasty bug out of his mouth.

I asked my children, "Do you think the girl would have thought differently about the boy if she'd known about the bug?" They were sure she would have.

Then I shared that sometimes we *think* we know what's going on, but in reality we don't have the entire story. Too many times we make judgments about someone without all of the information.

There are days when I need to "spit a bug." An encounter with a rude sales clerk, an angry teen or fussy toddler may only be the tip of the iceberg. When I refuse to look deeper, I'm closing my heart off to the needs of others. Not surprisingly, I've found people are more responsive when I take time to get to the root of their sorrow.

Since I've started to "spit a bug," I've had several opportunities to encourage others where they really hurt. I've been able to share the grace that keeps all of us from swallowing lies.

!!! MOM TALK !!!

Are there times when someone thought the wrong thing about you based on inadequate information? Is there someone in your life right now you might be judging based on limited information? Make a "grace list" of people who are difficult to like. Ask the God who knows the details in their lives to bless them with His grace and love.

Soccer Mom Tip

If you're nervous about taking your newly potty-trained child out in public, try training diapers with larger underwear over the top. Your child will still feel like a big kid.

Did You Know?

The following are some lesser-known facts about some well-known people:

Walt Disney, film producer and co-founder of the Walt Disney Company: In 1964, Walt Disney Productions began quietly purchasing land in central Florida southwest of Orlando in a large swamp land for Disney's "Florida Project." Disney did so under the mask of many fake companies in order to keep the price of land as low as he could. As soon as the word got out that Disney was purchasing the land, however, the prices immediately rose.

James Dobson, Founder of Focus on the Family Ministries: After his bestselling book *Bringing Up Boys* found its way into millions of homes, Dobson decided to publish *Bringing Up Girls*. During his research process he humbly admitted, "Girls are a lot more complex than boys." (Don't we all know that one!)

Debbie Macomber, *New York Times* bestselling author: With more than 60 million books in print, Macomber's book *A Good Yarn* inspired a Christian woman's domestic violence program to open a yarn shop called "A New Yarn." Debbie and her husband attended the Grand Opening and continue to support the ministry.

Henrietta Mears, evangelist: Not only was she a spiritual mentor to evangelist Billy Graham and Campus Crusade for Christ founder Bill Bright, but also she and a group of businessmen established Gospel Light Publications, one of the first publishers in the Christian education field.

Steven Spielberg, film director/producer: After moving to California, Steven Spielberg applied to attend film school at UCLA and the University of Southern California's School of Cinema-Television three separate times. He was not accepted due to his C grade average.

Mother Teresa, Nobel Peace Prize recipient: By the time she was 12, Agnes Gonxha Bojaxhiu was convinced that her vocation should be a religious life. She left her home at age 18 to join the Sisters of Loreto as a missionary. Agnes, later called Mother Teresa, would never again set eyes on her mother or sister.

Margaret Thatcher, former British prime minister: Margaret Thatcher worked as a research chemist for J. Lyons and Co., where she helped develop methods for preserving ice cream. She was a member of the team that developed the first soft frozen ice cream.

Oprah Winfrey, talk-show host: Winfrey's grandmother taught her to read before the age of three and took her to the local church, where she was nicknamed "The Preacher" for her ability to recite Bible verses.

Orville Wright, aviator: In 1878, Orville's father, who traveled often as a bishop in the Church of the United Brethren in Christ, brought home a toy "helicopter" for his two younger sons. Wilbur and Orville played with it until it broke, and then built their own. In later years, they pointed to their experience with the toy as the initial spark of their interest in flying.

Source: Walt Disney: http://en.wikipedia.org/wiki/Walt_disney; James Dobson: Focus on the Family (direct quote), September 2007; Debbie Macomber: personal correspondence from author, September 2007; Henrietta Mears: http://en.wikipedia.org/wiki/Henrietta_Mears; Steven Spielberg: http://en.wikipedia.org/wiki/Steven_Spielberg; Mother Teresa: http://en.wikipedia.org/wiki/Mother_Teresa; Margaret Thatcher: http://en.wikipedia.org/wiki/Margaret_thatcher; Oprah Winfrey: http://en.wikipedia.org/wiki/Oprah_Winfrey; Orville Wright: http://en.wikipedia.org/wiki/Orville_Wright\.

Mom's Space

God: Do not judge, or you too will be judged. In the same way you judge others, you will be judged, and with the measure you use, it will be measured to you (see Matthew 7:1-2).

Mom:

_____

_____

_____

_____

_____

_____

_____

_____

_____

_____

God: Be kind and compassionate to one another and forgive each other, just as in Christ I forgave you (see Ephesians 4:32).

Mom:

_____

_____

_____

_____

_____

_____

_____

_____

2

2

COMMUNION

Sometimes I do the wrong things. Many times I say the wrong things, and quite often I think the wrong things.

It's with this realization that I woke up one Sunday morning. I felt so worthless and frustrated with my inability to overcome and live a life totally obedient to God. I went to church anyway and, as luck would have it, it was Communion Sunday with the junior high group.

I sat in the dimly lit chapel wondering if I should partake of the bread and cup, considering my pitiful attitude about failing to meet God's perfect standard. I started to make my way up to the front where the pastor had placed a loaf of bread and a wine glass filled with Welch's juice.

Then I heard it: The shattering of glass and a gasp from those in the front row. A student had accidentally knocked over the glass, leaving a puddle on the newly installed carpet. I ran for the paper towels. In a matter of minutes, I was on my knees with another youth worker drying up juice and picking up pieces of broken glass . . . and then I traveled back in time.

My mind envisioned that day when my freedom from sin was won. I saw my Savior dying on a cruel wooden cross, His blood pouring out as payment to purchase sinners—sinners that could never earn their way to perfection. It was so real. I could almost hear His voice: *I know you aren't perfect. That's why I came. Father, forgive them.*

Now, I'm not part of a liturgical church community, so the whole concept of the Eucharist has always eluded me. But not that day. That Sunday I was on my knees sopping up my Savior's blood. He was there in the wine. He was there for me.

> *"For I received from the Lord what I also*
> *passed on to you: The Lord Jesus,*
> *on the night he was betrayed, took bread,*
> *and when he had given thanks, he broke it and said,*
> *'This is my body, which is for you; do this in*
> *remembrance of me.' In the same way,*
> *after supper he took the cup, saying,*
> *'This cup is the new covenant in my blood;*
> *do this, whenever you drink it, in remembrance of me.'*
> *For whenever you eat this bread and drink this cup,*
> *you proclaim the Lord's death until he comes."*

The Apostle Paul (1 Corinthians 11:23-26)

!!! MOM TALK !!!

What are the sins you struggle with? What keeps you from accepting the forgiveness given to you in Christ Jesus? Write those sins down on a piece of paper, and ask God to forgive you and make you clean again. Then toss the paper in the nearest trashcan. Those sins can haunt you no longer. You are forgiven.

 Soccer Mom Tip
Make Bible stories come alive by creating a hand puppet out of a tube sock to tell the story.

Christ's Sacrifice

Because of our Lord's sacrifice, our sins are:

- **Forgiven:** "All the prophets testify about him that everyone who believes in him [Jesus Christ] receives forgiveness of sins through his name" (Acts 10:43).

- **Wiped Out:** "Repent, then, and turn to God, so that your sins may be wiped out, that times of refreshing may come from the Lord" (Acts 3:19)

- **Washed Away:** "And now what are you waiting for? Get up, be baptized and wash your sins away, calling on his name"(Acts 22:16).

- **Covered:** "Blessed are they whose transgressions are forgiven, whose sins are covered" (Romans 4:7).

- **Taken Away:** "And this is my covenant with them when I take away their sins" (Romans 11:27).

- **Forgotten:** "For I will forgive their wickedness and will remember their sins no more" (Hebrews 8:12).

- **Gone:** "But if we walk in the light, as he is in the light, we have fellowship with one another, and the blood of Jesus, his Son, purifies us from all sin" (1 John 1:7).

 # Mom's Space

God: In Christ you have a ransom paid through His blood, the forgiveness of your sins, according to the riches of My grace (see Ephesians 1:7).

Mom:

_____

_____

_____

_____

_____

_____

_____

_____

God: I am He who blots out your sins, for My own sake. I do not remember your sins anymore (see Isaiah 43:35).

Mom:

_____

_____

_____

_____

_____

_____

Soccer
Momism

"*I'm so proud of you!*"

BROKEN TOY

After my son's first week at preschool, he told me that he had met a girl there who was a broken doll.

"What do you mean?" I asked.

He explained that she wore a patch on her eye, so she was kind of like a broken toy. He also added that he didn't want to be friends with her. I figured that he was kind of scared of the patch. Then I asked him a question.

"Does she know that you are broken, too?"

"I'm not broken," he announced.

"Yes, you are. You have a bad food allergy and that makes you broken."

His eyes widened. "Oh."

"Besides," I added, "everyone is broken. Some are broken on the outside like your sweet doll friend, and others are broken on the inside like you. Everyone needs to be fixed by a patch, medicine or even a doctor. But there's one kind of brokenness that only God can fix."

"What kind is that?"

"A heart that refuses to be friends with others. Only God can heal that."

I waited and then asked my son if he wanted to ask Jesus to fix his broken heart so that he would be able to love other broken people just like him. He decided that was a good idea. We bowed our heads and prayed, and I have to admit I felt some of that healing power going on inside of me, too.

!!! MOM TALK !!!

In what ways are you broken? Who are the broken people in your life? How can you show them love in their brokenness?

 Soccer Mom Tip
When you see gifts on sale, buy two and store the extra in a "gift closet" for times when you need a present and don't have time to shop. Stock up on tissue paper and gift bags of various sizes.

Helping Your Child Embrace Those with Special Needs

- **Alleviate the Fear:** Make sure your child understands that the disability is not like a cold that can be caught.

- **Let Them Look:** Telling a child not to stare at the person is unreasonable—after all, investigating is how kids learn. Instead verbalize what your child is doing: "Are you noticing that brace? That's interesting isn't it? I bet it helps that person walk better."

- **Channel Inquisitiveness:** Ask your child if she wants to go over with you to ask the person questions (if it's okay with his or her helper).

- **Assume the Person with the Disability Can Understand:** If there are communication problems, the caregiver can interpret.

- **Encourage Role-play:** Allow your child the freedom to act out the disability at home. It is completely normal for children to mimic what they see, but don't allow the mimicry to become fodder for a cruel joke.

- **Provide Further Discussion at Home Regarding Disabilities:** Allow your child self-expression through art, music or drama.

- **Invite a Special-needs Child to Your Home for a Fun Event:** Ask his or her caregiver how the event can best work. Consider holding a play-date at the other child's home.

Source: Lynne M. Thompson, "Just Like Me," interview with Jon Ebersole, Director for the Chicago area of Joni and Friends, 2004.

Mom's Space

God: Who gave people their mouths? Who makes them deaf or mute? Who gives them sight or makes them blind? Is it not I, the Lord (see Exodus 4:11)?

Mom:

_____

_____

_____

_____

_____

_____

_____

_____

God: My grace is sufficient for you, because My power is made perfect in weakness (see 2 Corinthians 12:9).

Mom:

_____

_____

_____

_____

_____

_____

_____

_____

FREE LUNCH

The other day my son placed two dollars on my desk and instructed me to put it into his account. I asked him where he got the money.

"This one boy didn't want his school lunch, so he gave it to me and went out to recess. Since I couldn't eat two lunches, I sold his lunch to another kid for two bucks."

I was flabbergasted. Mostly because school lunches cost $1.50 and my son had just sold his overstock for more than the market rate. I explained that it's probably against school rules to sell wholesale lunches at retail prices.

"Look," he explained, "these people have money to burn on things like candy and video games, so why shouldn't I sell them something like extra lunches?"

"I know, honey, but you sold them something they could have gotten cheaper in the lunch line."

He agreed in the future that he would sell the lunch at the going rate. I clarified that he wasn't a food broker and should stick to the books for now. He can run a food company later . . . like, after grammar school.

This whole event reminded me of another character in the Bible who tried to buy something that was already free: Simon the Sorcerer, who tried to buy the power of the Holy Spirit.

Simon had followed the apostle Philip around Samaria for some time, and Simon was very impressed. For years the multitudes had been mesmerized by Simon's magical powers, but now the people were following Philip and being baptized in the name of Jesus. Simon decided that he, too, would be baptized.

The apostles Peter and John visited Samaria and began placing their hands on the new believers so that they might receive the Holy Spirit. Again, Simon was very impressed. So much so that he decided to invest his capital in this awesome power. The only problem? God was not for sale.

Peter called Simon on his hypocrisy and suggested that he repent of his wickedness, because obviously Simon hadn't been paying attention. Phillip and the other apostles weren't participating in multilevel marketing, or some kind of pyramid scheme. No, they were fulfilling what Christ had commanded them to do: "Go and make disciples of all nations, baptizing them in the name of the Father and of the Son and of the Holy Spirit" (Matthew 28:19). They weren't to collect any fees for this gift because God had already paid for it.

In our day of mass marketing and consumerism, it's refreshing to know that you and I, regardless of our economic status, may still receive life's most precious gift. And best of all, it is free.

If you have never asked the Savior into your life, today can be your day to receive God's greatest gift.

> *Dear God, Thank You for sending Your Son to die on the cross for my sins. You knew that I could never be good enough to enter Your kingdom, so You paid my way. I now give my life over to You as a living sacrifice.*

I want to do things Your way. Come into me, Holy
Spirit, and direct my path in the way everlasting.

!!! MOM TALK !!!

Has God done something that has impressed you? When did
you receive God's free gift? The Holy Spirit is alive in every
believer. Ask Him to move in your life in a mighty way this
very day.

 Soccer Mom Tip
When your child is angry, redirect energy bursts
into positive outlets like running, jumping, blowing into a horn or painting.

Sack Lunch Menu Planner

Monday	Tuesday	Wednesday	Thursday	Friday
Aram sandwich	Egg salad on bread	Turkey sandwich	Tuna on croisant	Lunch meat in rolled tortilla
Apples and peanut butter	Banana chips	Cheese sticks	Soy chips	Trail mix
Jello	Fruit Roll	Orange	Grapes	Snap peas and carrots with Ranch dressing

Mom's Space

God: For it is by grace you have been saved, through faith, not something you earned. It is My gift (see Ephesians 3:20).

Mom:

_____

_____

_____

_____

_____

_____

_____

_____

God: I am able to do immeasurably more than all you ask or imagine, according to My power that is at work in you (see Ephesians 2:8).

Mom:

_____

_____

_____

_____

_____

_____

_____

Soccer Momism

"Who needs to go potty?"

25

TODAY

It is time. The bandage that once provided protection on my little one's tanned knee is no longer needed. The wound has healed. Unfortunately, the adhesive has firmly attached itself to the tender skin surrounding the injury.

I have two options. I can *appear* gentle by gingerly prying the bandage off, or I can *seem* cruel, ripping that puppy off with one quick jerk. Either way, it will hurt.

I decide that quicker is the more merciful of the two.

Each time I do this, of course, I'm rewarded with that same look of betrayal on my child's face. He believes me to be mean, which I'm not. I'm doing him a favor, even if he doesn't see it that way.

Then I remember the times when life throws me a curve. I never see it coming; it happens all too fast. And I catch myself giving God that same look. At first I believe that God is cruel: He didn't jump in and help me the way I thought He should. In hindsight, though, I can always see that His way was best. The pain was used for an ultimate good in my life.

In my son's case, a few hours later he crawls into my lap, forgiving me for my apparent cruelty. I think he finally realizes that Mommy wouldn't do anything that wasn't covered in love.

Then I look up toward heaven and realize that my Lord would do no less than the same. I will never realize the lingering pain He's saved me from. I need to crawl into my heavenly Father's lap. It is time.

!!! MOM TALK !!!

How has God protected you in your life? What kinds of things has God allowed into your life that you wouldn't have chosen?

Soccer Mom Tip
If your child is receiving unwanted physical attention at school, try acting out a scene together, giving him the words needed to set boundaries.

Did You Know a Covered Wound . . .

- **Heals more efficiently:** Bandages that absorb the fluid of a wound and maintain a natural moisture balance are ideal for healing.

- **Decreases the chance of scarring:** Keeping a wound covered until it heals can prevent a scab from forming, thereby minimizing chances of scarring.

- **Has less chance of infection:** Bandages help prevent exposure to water, dirt and germs.

- **Enjoys superior protection:** Bandages provide extra cushioning for added comfort and protection from re-injury until the wound is completely healed.

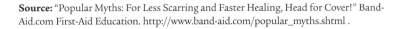

Source: "Popular Myths: For Less Scarring and Faster Healing, Head for Cover!" Band-Aid.com First-Aid Education. http://www.band-aid.com/popular_myths.shtml .

Mom's Space

God: I know the plans I have for you. Plans to prosper you and not to harm you, plans to give you hope and a future (see Jeremiah 29:11).

Mom:

_____

_____

_____

_____

_____

_____

_____

_____

_____

_____

God: I have taken you to the banquet hall, and My banner over you is love (see Song of Songs 2:4).

Mom:

_____

_____

_____

_____

_____

_____

_____

_____

26

THE PORCELAIN DOLL

Like most kindergarten boys, there's a bit of elfish mischief in my son that revels in making his sister jump, scream and run frantically from whatever torture tool he flashes, such as a snail or water balloon.

But for the most part, my two children are inseparable. Bunk beds become secret forts, pinkie promises are sacred and treats are to be divided 50-50. But even with so much friendship between them, nothing could have prepared me for the small act of kindness my son, David, expressed one Christmas.

It was a windy day in December when David and I attended the all-school Christmas boutique. I shoved a dollar into his hand and told him to go shopping. Only two minutes later he came back with a sack holding his purchase: It was a beautiful porcelain doll he'd purchased for his sister.

There are not words to express how proud I was of my son, who had spent his only dollar on his sister, and got a bargain to boot.

I only wish the story ended there.

On the way to the car, I heard the crash. David sobbed as he scooped the doll out of the gutter, her feet lying shattered in pieces on the ground.

I knew there was no fixing her, but I promised that with booties on her feet, no one would notice the difference.

When Christmas morning arrived, I pulled my daughter aside and explained to her about the gift and how it was accidentally broken. I asked her to love it anyway.

God has to continually tap me on the shoulder and say, "Be gentle with your fellow man; he has flaws, personality defects borne out of a shattered life, but his heart wants so badly to contribute something of value."

Everything went as planned. My daughter was grateful and my son beamed with joy. I ran to get the camera, in hopes of capturing this holiday moment. As I focused through the lens on my two children, I blinked in disbelief. Slowly moving the camera away from my eye, I gazed upon the doll's face. I had never noticed before, but her eyes were painted closed.

Blinded by love, overflowing with grace.

Isn't that what Christmas is all about?

!!! Mom Talk !!!

What are your pet peeves? What habits do you have that may annoy others? Who are the people God has placed into your life who need your gentleness?

 Soccer Mom Tip

If you need your child to be on time, give small specific steps. Instead of "I want you ready in 10 minutes," try "I want you to put on your shoes and coat and stand here."

Christmas Quiz

What really happened that Christmas night? Take this test and see if you can discern fact from fiction.

True or False:

_____ The account of Jesus' birth is in the book of John.

_____ Joseph and Mary traveled to the town of Nazareth.

_____ An angel of the Lord appeared to Joseph in a dream and told him about Jesus.

_____ Mary put straw in the manger for baby Jesus.

_____ Mary knew she was having a boy.

_____ Three wise men came to the manger scene.

_____ Jesus, our bread of life, was born in a town that translated means "house of bread."

(See answers on page 191.)

# Mom's Space

God: As My chosen people, holy and dearly loved, clothe yourselves with compassion, kindness, humility, gentleness and patience (see Colossians 3:12).

Mom:

_____

_____

_____

_____

_____

_____

_____

God: Let your gentleness be evident to all. I am near (see Philippians 4:5).

Mom:

_____

_____

_____

_____

_____

_____

_____

THE MESSAGE

It was tree-chopping day at the school. My children and I walked thought the bits and pieces of debris, leftovers from the grinding machine.

Then we saw it: One lonely tree stood by itself bearing a sign wrapped around its trunk that read, "Don't chop me down. I am loved." I smiled. Obviously this person's plea to save their forest friend was heeded. This tree was valuable because someone loved it.

During the month of January, many celebrate the sanctity of human life. Yet there are also a great number of people who claim to be pro-choice and support their position by stating that it's not right to bring an unwanted or "unloved" child into the world.

They must have missed the sign. Stamped into every human embryo, fetus and baby, there is a plea from our Creator to value human life. In fact, His message is quite personal.

In case you missed it, here it is:

God created man in his own image, in the image of God he created him (Genesis 1:27).

My prayer is that someday we will live in a world where this sign will be respected.

!!! Mom Talk !!!

Do you know someone who thinks that they are not valuable? Are there times in your life when you have felt worthless? To God, you are a priceless work of art. You are so valuable that only God Himself was worthy enough to purchase you. Now you are on display as His beautiful handiwork.

 Soccer Mom Tip
Provide ways for your child to meet new friends. Have the church group over for a jewelry-making or Lego-building party, or invite new friends over for pizza and a movie.

Nine Ways You Can Be a "Life Buddy" for Your Pastor

1. Keep your pastor on the cutting edge by emailing news articles on life issues.
2. Become a liaison with your local crisis pregnancy center (CPC) and report special events and opportunities to serve.
3. Introduce your pastor to possible fundraising opportunities for your local CPC.
4. Host baby showers for moms in crisis pregnancies.
5. Pray with your pastor on a regular basis regarding life issues.
6. Assist your church's staff with scheduling pro-life speakers to visit your church.
7. Take baby items, donated by the congregation, to your local CPC.
8. Help your pastor plan a special service for Sanctity of Life Sunday, which is held in January.
9. Offer information regarding pro-life issues during the announcement time on Sunday.

Mom's Space

God: I created your innermost being; I knit you together in your mother's womb (see Psalm 139:13).

Mom:

God: Put on your new self, the one that is being renewed to a true knowledge, according to My image, the One who created you (see Colossians 3:10).

Mom:

Soccer Momism
"Clean your room!"

28

WAITING

Do you feel like you're on eternal hold? That's what I say when referring to those companies that put my phone call on hold for several minutes at a time. I say this jokingly, but honestly there are times in my life when I feel like God has placed me on hold and forgotten me there.

Is God ignoring my prayers? Doesn't He hear my cries for His help?

I'm reminded of a group of fishermen that asked Jesus the same question. The wind became fierce and waves broke over their boat, threatening to capsize it. The disciples woke Jesus up and said to Him, "Teacher, don't You care if we drown?"

Our groggy Lord sat up and commanded the waves to be still. And they obeyed! Then Jesus rebuked the men, asking them, "Why are you so afraid? Do you still have no faith?" (Mark 4:40).

Ouch.

That event gives me new perspective. I don't need to be afraid. When things are at their worst, my God will calm the storms in my life. After all, He has the power to take care of whatever tragic events come my way. Now *that's* comforting.

But while I'm waiting, I think I'll program faith into my speed dial.

!!! MOM TALK !!!

What prayer are you currently waiting on God to answer? Name a time when God answered a prayer in a way you hadn't anticipated. In what ways is this "holding time" increasing your faith in God?

Soccer Mom Tip

Teach your child matching by using computer clipart. Create a sheet with animals, household items, letters or numbers. Print two copies, cut out the objects on the first sheet, and have your child glue them onto the matching picture on the second.

What's Your Record Time on Hold?

- ❏ Under 2 minutes

- ❏ 5-10 minutes (I painted my nails.)

- ❏ 15-25 minutes (I did the dishes.)

- ❏ 30 minutes (I paid all of my bills.)

- ❏ 50 minutes (I cleaned the bathrooms.)

- ❏ Over 1 hour (I cleaned my entire house and took a nap.)

- ❏ I'm still on hold.

Mom's Space

God: Wait patiently for Me; I will turn to you and hear your cry. I will lift you out of the slimy pit, out of the mud and mire; I will set your feet on a rock and give you a firm place to stand (see Psalm 40:1-2).

Mom:

_____

_____

_____

_____

_____

_____

_____

_____

God: The salvation of the righteous comes from Me. I am your stronghold in times of trouble (see Psalm 37:9).

Mom:

_____

_____

_____

_____

_____

_____

_____

_____

Soccer Momism

"I just bought you a pair of shoes!"

29

CLEAN ROOM

Today was the quarterly Cleaning of the Rooms. To give you a sense of the scope of this project, in the past I've had to contact the sanitation department to schedule a trash bin delivery.

My son's room looks like a manufacturing plant, scattered with body parts of his precious Bionicle toys. Next door, my daughter's floor is carpeted with several layers of recently purchased junior apparel. Both of them seem to have an obsession with trash, though no one knows how it got there. A mystery indeed. Perhaps there is some magnetic field located in each of their rooms that sucks in all unclaimed garbage. Yeah, that's gotta be it.

I'd like to report to you that in minutes everything is cleaned up neat as a pin, and we sit and eat cookies and milk on the back patio while the birds sing sweetly in the trees above. But that would be a huge lie. No, C-Day is filled with anguish, excuses and tears. Sort of like the times I clean my most important room—my heart.

On cleaning day, the passage in Scripture that speaks of putting "childish ways behind me" (1 Corinthians 13:11) becomes very real. It's hard to part with things I think I need—things like television or computers, which can rob me of my time with the Lord, or the quest for the latest clothing item that will never satisfy my desire to look more important.

Eventually there are excuses about how things got so messed up in my spiritual room to begin with. "I was too busy." "I was tired." "I had better things to do." Just like my children need me to come in and help them sort through all the "stuff," I call upon my Lord, who is right there with His truck, hauling out the things that get in the way of our relationship. And then the tears come. In this case, tears of repentance and joy. I have the opportunity to start fresh. My heart is clean.

!!! MOM TALK !!!

What is the one area in your home that is the messiest? What kinds of things do you need God to clean up in your heart? Schedule a cleaning appointment with the Lord. Take a day to meet with Him about the areas in your life that need sorting out.

> **Soccer Mom Tip**
> Go over the rules for craft activities before you start. For example, "Crayons never go in our ears or our mouth" or "Clay dough only stays on the mat." Talk about clean-up before you ever begin.

Room Cleaning Tips for Kids

Make a donation. Box up outgrown or unwanted items like clothing, toys or games. They take up valuable space. If you find you still have too much, hold a "favorites" contest. Lay out all the pants, shirts, toys and so on, and pick the top 10; donate the rest to a mission or shelter.

Store seasonal things. Hats, gloves and sweaters can be stored in plastic containers during the summer and kept in the attic or under a bed. The same goes for swimwear and shorts in the winter.

Give it a home. Everything in the room should have a designated place. A box for jewelry, a tower for CDs and DVDs, a sports bag for athletic equipment, a box for crafts, a bin for school books, a basket for trash. Remember to assign one "junk drawer" for things that don't belong anywhere else.

Box the shoes. Instead of ditching shoeboxes, keep them in the closet to store shoes.

Hang it up. It's easier to see what to wear when it's in front of you. Organize shirts and jeans by color, and leave the dresser drawers for undergarments, play clothes, pajamas and accessory items.

Decorate with shelves. Display those stuffed animals and mementoes above, where they are out of the way and off the floor.

Ditch the clothes hamper. Instead, deposit clothing in the laundry room or in a basket in the garage. The room will smell nicer, and you can walk on carpet—not clothes.

Mount a board. Affix a magnetic board or corkboard to the back of your child's bedroom door, where messages and notes can be posted.

Do a TMT. Once a day, perform a Ten-Minute Tidy. Set the timer and move misplaced items where they belong.

Celebrate! After the room is finished, take time to lie down on a clean bed and soak in the beauty of an organized room. It's the perfect opportunity to remind your child that we serve a God of order who put everything in the right place for His divine purposes.

Mom's Space

God: Come now, let us reason together. Though your sins are like scarlet, they shall be white as snow; though they are red as crimson, they shall be like wool (see Isaiah 1:18).

Mom:

_____

_____

_____

_____

_____

_____

_____

_____

God: Don't lose heart. Though outwardly you are wasting away, inwardly you are being renewed day by day (see 2 Corinthians 4:16).

Mom:

_____

_____

_____

_____

_____

_____

_____

Soccer
Momism
"You need a bath."

BUNNY PSYCHOLOGY

One day, I looked over at Prince Charming, our fluffy white Holland Lop bunny, and felt guilty. He resides in a large cage, and other than his PVC tube, he had no comfortable place to lie down. I reasoned that it couldn't be pleasant to have wires as your mattress, so I took a trip to the local dollar store and picked up a rubber sink mat. *That ought to do the trick.*

This, I knew, was definitely going to improve his quality of life. So I placed the mat in his favorite resting spot, and he . . . grabbed it with his front teeth and lobbed it to the other side of the cage. How ungrateful!

I tried again, thinking he must not have liked the location of the mat. This time he started eating it. Yikes! That couldn't be good for him. I quickly removed my chewed-up mat, thankful I was only out a buck.

I whined to my husband that Prince was an ungrateful and foolish rabbit. Here I was actually trying to make his life better, and that's the thanks I got? That's when my husband spouted these words of wisdom: "He has to realize his need before you can help him, and obviously Prince Charming doesn't think he needs a new mattress."

"Then how can we help him?" I asked.

My husband smiled and said, "The day might come when Prince will see his need. Trials hit us all."

I paused and began reflecting on some of the people in my life who don't think they need God's help at all. But someday hardship will visit them, and I'll be there, not with judgment, but with a helping hand.

!!! MOM TALK !!!

When has it been difficult for you to receive help from someone else? Who do you know that claims not to need God's help? What acts of kindness can you display when this person is ready?

 Soccer Mom Tip

If bad weather has you stuck inside, take time for Sock Wars. Grab a bunch of rolled up socks and run for cover! Kids love to hide and pelt each other (and you) with a sock ball. To avoid any collisions, play on your knees.

People Who Discovered Their Need for God

Who	Crisis Situation
Abram	He and his wife were old and without an heir (see Genesis 15:3).
Jacob	He believed his brother's army was on its way to destroy him and his family (see Genesis 32:11).

Joseph	He was thrown into prison and forgotten (see Genesis 39:20).
Moses	He was exiled for killing an Egyptian (see Exodus 2:14-15).
Samson	He was blinded and enslaved (see Judges 16:21).
Queen of Sheba	She lacked wisdom (see 1 Kings 10:8).
The Widow	She and her son were starving until Elijah came (see 1 Kings 17:12).
Children of Israel	They were enslaved by the Babylonians (see Jeremiah 52:28-30).
Jonah	He was thrown overboard and swallowed by a fish (see Jonah 1:17).
Adulterous Woman	She was about to be stoned to death (see John 8:3-5).
Roman Centurion	His servant became paralyzed and needed healing from Jesus (see Matthew 8:6).
Saul of Tarsus	He became blind and stood accused by God as a persecutor of the Church (see Acts 9:5-8).

Mom's Space

God: A person finds joy in giving an appropriate reply—and how good is a timely word (see Proverbs 15:23)!

Mom:

_____

_____

_____

_____

_____

_____

_____

_____

_____

God: Preach the Word; be prepared in season and out of season; correct, rebuke and encourage—with great patience and careful instruction (2 Timothy 4:2).

Mom:

_____

_____

_____

_____

_____

_____

_____

_____

31

THE TWO MARYS

We had an interesting predicament this last Christmas. One of my dear friends gave us a nativity scene made of beautifully painted ceramic. Each of the characters' faces was quite animated and lovely. But as we set up the blessed scene on one of my tables, we noticed something rather peculiar. There were two Marys.

I called my friend to make sure she hadn't given another set that lacked the mother of our Lord to someone else. She indicated that she hadn't and that we were welcome to keep the extra Mary.

My daughter quickly confiscated the figurine and carried it to her room. It occurred to me how appropriate it was that Mary go to Cassie, my soon-to-be teenager. After all, Mary was herself only a teen.

I pondered on that night so long ago when an innocent young girl, excited about her future independence as a wife and freedom from parental authority, was told that her life was not going to be what she expected. Her dreams would be altered. Her peers would ridicule her. She would stand out from all the rest. Her reputation would be destroyed.

Mary's body was not her own—the Holy Spirit would come upon her and the power of the Most High would overshadow her.

In response, there wasn't rebellion from Mary, but resolve: "I am the Lord's servant. May it be to me as you have said" (Luke 1:38).

Yes, Mary is definitely the kind of teen I want hanging out in my daughter's room.

!!! MOM TALK !!!

What kind of friends do your children have? How do your own friends influence your walk with God? What kind of influence do you have on those around you?

> **Soccer Mom Tip**
> Take your child out for community service projects. Visit a convalescent home or collect food cans in the neighborhood for a homeless shelter.

Does Your Friend Pass the Character Filter?

Is she divisive or a gossip? Proverbs 16:28: "A perverse man stirs up dissension, and a gossip separates close friends."

Is she easily angered? Proverbs 16:29: "A violent man entices his neighbor and leads him down a path that is not good."

Does she ignore good advice? Proverbs 12:15: "The way of a fool seems right to him, but a wise man listens to advice."

Does she lie? Proverbs 12:22: "The Lord detests lying lips, but he delights in men who are truthful."

Does she admit her mistakes? Proverbs 15:12: "A mocker resents correction; he will not consult the wise."

Is she greedy? Proverbs 15:27: "A greedy man brings trouble to his family, but he who hates bribes will live."

Does she constantly flatter you? Proverbs 29:5: "Whoever flatters his neighbor is spreading a net for his feet."

 # Mom's Space

God: Do not be misled: Bad company corrupts good character (see 1 Corinthians 15:33).

Mom:

_____

_____

_____

_____

_____

_____

_____

_____

God: As iron sharpens iron, so one man sharpens another (see Proverbs 27:17).

Mom:

_____

_____

_____

_____

_____

_____

_____

_____

Soccer Momism
"Where will you be?"

32

LOST BOY

"I can't find him."

The four words no mom wants to hear, especially at a large amusement park. My son had been playing in one spot and now he was gone. We called out his name, continuing the search with the assistance of park employees. Gates were secured; a shutdown was set in motion.

Fear started making it's way through my entire body, threatening to paralyze me with its lies. I was familiar with the voice. It's the same one that speaks to me when I'm asked to do something difficult or when my seemingly organized world begins to fall apart. The message never changes; it's always the same: *God is not in charge.*

Now, I've read most of the Scriptures and sat through many sermons, but never once have I been taught that God is not in control. Sure, things don't always go the way I think they should, but He is always in charge. Even now.

So, I decided to ignore the lie. I listened to God's Spirit speak truth. "Never will I leave you; never will I forsake you" (Hebrews 13:5). No matter what happened, I wasn't going to fall out of His tight grip. God's love for me is too great to ever let go.

Finally, we found my son, playing in another area not too far from where we'd left him. I hugged and scolded, "God sure is increasing my faith with you, son."

He smiled and replied, "Then I should keep on doing this."

"Don't even go there," my husband warned.

I smiled. Too late. God had already been there, just like always.

!!! Mom Talk !!!

When have you felt deserted by God? How have you allowed God to use that event in your life to make you more like Him? Take time to thank God for His plans and for never leaving you.

 Soccer Mom Tip

When you visit relatives or friends, remember that their homes are not necessarily childproof.

Park Survival

Here are a few tips on how to keep track of your children when hitting a crowded park.

- Stake out a designated meeting place before you start your day that will be easy for your child to remember.
- Tell your child to ask a clerk behind a cash register for assistance if he or she becomes lost.
- Consider placing younger children on a wrist leash to allow for some freedom.
- Use masking tape to put your cell phone number on the outside of your child's clothing.
- Make sure older children have cell phones with them at all times, and meet throughout the day to regroup.
- Communicate that under no circumstances is any one allowed to leave the park without a parent.
- Utilize the buddy system, and make sure that no one goes to the bathroom alone.

Mom's Space

God: I am your refuge and strength, an ever-present help in trouble (see Psalm 46:1).

Mom:

_____

_____

_____

_____

_____

_____

_____

_____

_____

God: Take refuge in Me and be glad; sing for joy. I will spread my protection over you (see Psalm 5:11).

Mom:

_____

_____

_____

_____

_____

_____

_____

_____

THE RABBIT SHOW

I had never been to a rabbit show before. My daughter's new-found hobby placed our family right in the middle of Bunny Central. The annual show boasted over 40 different breeds, and judging by the sea of cages before me, there was a whole lot of bunny lovin' going on.

Our family meandered through the makeshift aisles until a kind gentleman took pity and adopted us for the day. I proudly pointed to our Holland Lop rabbit.

"Don't you think our bunny will win? He's so cute," I boasted.

The man smiled. "Well, if cuteness was how they were judged, then you'd definitely have a chance, but that's not how they do it here."

"They don't? How do they judge?" I asked.

"By *Rabbit and Cavie Standards*."

"The what?" I'd never heard of such a thing.

"It's a book," he explained. "It lists all of the standards and ideals for each breed. You've never read it?"

I bit my lip. "Umm, no."

"Gee, that's too bad," he said. "Your rabbit will be judged by it whether you've read it or not."

I looked at my bunny again. Funny, I'd never noticed his crooked ear before. In light of the standard, I knew he wouldn't fare well. Then I saw my daughter reach out and hug her bunny. She held him close to her chest and kissed him on the nose. She wasn't about to let something like a standard determine her love.

Our rabbit still lives with us today. We've named him Prince Charming. He reminds us of another Prince—Jesus, the Prince of Peace—who came to rescue mankind from a harsh and unattainable standard.

!!! Mom Talk !!!

In what ways do you fall short of God's standard of perfection? What are some ways you bestow God's grace on your family? Sing for joy! God has freed you from your sin. In Christ, you will not be judged.

> ### ⚽ Soccer Mom Tip
> Does your child have a hero who has disappointed him? Have your child send an encouraging note to a fallen athlete or star, promising to lift that person up in prayer—then be sure to follow through.

The Ten Commandments

I. No other gods, only me.

II. No carved gods of any size, shape or form of anything whatever, whether of things that fly or walk or swim. Don't bow down to them and don't serve them because *I* am God, your God, and I'm a most jealous God, punishing the children for any sins their parents pass on to them to the third, and yes, even to the fourth generation of those who hate me. But I'm unswervingly loyal to the thousands who love me and keep my commandments.

III. No using the name of GOD, your GOD, in curses or silly banter; GOD won't put up with the irreverent use of His name.

IV. Observe the Sabbath day. Keep it holy. Work six days and do everything you need to do. But the seventh day is a Sabbath to GOD, your GOD. No one is to do any work—not you, your son, your daughter, your servant, your maid, your animals, or even the foreign guest visiting in your town. For in six days GOD made heaven, Earth, and the sea, and everything in them; He rested on the seventh day. Therefore GOD blessed the Sabbath day; He set it apart as a holy day.

V. Honor your father and mother so you'll live a long time in the land that GOD, your GOD, is giving you.

VI. No murder.

VII. No adultery.

VIII. No stealing.

IX. No lies about your neighbor.

X. No lusting after your neighbor's house—or wife, servant, maid, ox or donkey. Don't set your heart on anything that is your neighbor's (see Exodus 20:1-17, *THE MESSAGE*).

Mom's Space

God: Blessed is the person whose sin I do not count against him and in whose spirit is no deceit (see Psalm 32:2).

Mom:

_____

_____

_____

_____

_____

_____

_____

_____

God: I reconciled the world to myself in Christ, not counting your sins against you. You now have the message of reconciliation (see 2 Corinthians 5:19).

Mom:

_____

_____

_____

_____

_____

_____

_____

_____

Soccer
Momism
"Lights out!"

34

BAD COMPANY

It is impossible to live a life that is unaffected by other people. Their attitudes and opinions, like pollen, blow into our lives, shaping our perspective and influencing our decisions. When one godly person's life sharpens another's, it's a good thing. In time, it yields a harvest of mature fruit.

But I can think of several instances in my life when I allowed the negative influence of others to sway my better judgment. It started when I was young.

In grammar school: "Come on, we can sneak into the classroom without the teacher ever knowing." The teacher *did* know.

In high school: "Don't be such a drag. The toga party will be a blast!" With so much alcohol available, my friends couldn't remember what kind of party it was.

In college: "Let's get pizza. It won't hurt to skip class today." Unless, of course, the professor covers topics that weren't in the book, which he did.

As a young married woman: "Don't you think your husband is too tight with money?" He wasn't. But I didn't have enough discernment yet to realize that this older woman's suggestion was undermining my marriage.

The moments in which we've been swayed by someone's bad influence are often easier to see in retrospect. I'd like to think that as a "big girl" now, my judgment and perspective keep me from being so easily led astray. Unfortunately, I still have some blind spots, and I'm still vulnerable to being influenced toward ungodly attitudes and actions in some situations. The process can be so subtle that I don't even notice.

So now when I send my children out and tell them to make good choices about the friends they hang out with, I remind myself that the same goes for me.

!!! MOM TALK !!!

How are your children's friends influencing them? Who are the people you spend time with regularly? Are these people bringing you closer to or farther from God?

 Soccer Mom Tip

Have a family night once a week when everyone stays home to play a game, discuss a short passage in Scripture and enjoy a yummy dessert.

What to Do with Bad Influences

Set parameters. You might not have a problem spending time with this person in the office or at church, but you may need to forgo having contact with them outside of a group setting.

Distance yourself. You may need to distance yourself for a time to decide how to best handle this person's negative influence.

Flee. There are times when the desires of the flesh run strong and drastic measures are necessary. In those moments, we are not told to stay and witness, but to get out.

 Mom's Space

God: Be on your guard so that you may not be carried away by the error of lawless people and fall from your secure position (see 2 Peter 3:17).

Mom:

_____

_____

_____

_____

_____

_____

_____

_____

God: Do not envy wicked men, do not desire their company (Proverbs 24:1).

Mom:

_____

_____

_____

_____

_____

_____

_____

_____

35

Soccer
Momism
*"Do you want to talk
about it?"*

PERFECTION

I have a picky child. He is what we Thompsons call "H. M.," which stands for "high maintenance." His clothes have to be a certain way—and because most of the clothes hanging in his closet miss his stamp of approval, he ends up wearing pretty much the same thing every week. His hair must be just *so*— which means that on many days he spends more time in the bathroom than his teenage sister does. And his food—let's just say that many battles have been fought over the issue of food, battles I usually lose because, as all mothers know, you can't *make* a child eat.

I get so frustrated at times with his demand for perfection, and wonder where on earth it comes from. I start to scrutinize my own life to see if I've inadvertently communicated unrealistic goals. *Nah, it must be his father's fault.*

Okay, if I'm honest, I am guilty too. I realize there are many times I've chosen to focus on what *isn't* done at home, instead of what *is* done, or has at least been attempted. I'm quick to point out dirty dishes, shoes left out on the floor or weeds in the garden instead of noticing the way my son reaches out to others in kindness, finishes his homework on time or brings me joy just by being himself. I'm great at being a fault-finder.

Eventually, this tyrannical demand for everyone to snap to it and measure up leads me not to my cleaning closet, but to my knees. In no time at all, I realize that I'm greatly flawed and that I too miss the mark of perfection. I cry out to God for help, to release me from this cruel unreasonable yoke that I've placed on myself and others. And God shows up with great love and compassion.

Unlike me, He doesn't say, "Okay, I forgive you . . . but look at all the other areas you're messing up in!" No, instead He holds me tight and says, "It's okay. I love you, flaws and all." I'm reminded of a verse in Scripture that reads, "Be perfect, therefore, as your heavenly Father is perfect" (Matthew 5:48). My goal is to be perfectly forgiving and encouraging, just like my heavenly Father is to me.

!!! MOM TALK !!!

When was the last time you praised your child for a job well done? What are some unreasonable expectations you may be hanging on to? List some of the good things your family does and then plan a time to comment on those.

Soccer Mom Tip

Toddlers *can* enjoy a daily devotional time. Have it at approximately the same time each day, perhaps after breakfast or before snack. Reinforce the routine by calling your child with a Bible song, then read a story from a toddler-friendly Bible.

Food Recipes for the Picky Child

Pizza Sandwiches

Ingredients:
Sandwich bread
Spaghetti sauce in a jar
Thin slices of pepperoni, salami or ham
Grated Jack or cheddar cheese
Pineapple chunks

Directions: Spread a thin layer of spaghetti sauce on a slice of bread. Layer top with cheese, meat and pineapple chunks. Place in a 350°F oven and bake until cheese is melted. Cool slightly before eating.

Smoothies

Ingredients:
Frozen strawberries
Bananas
Flavored yogurt
Milk
Protein powder (No need to tell your child about this secret ingredient!)

Directions: Place desired amount into a blender and mix until smooth. Serve in a frosted glass with a straw.

Mom's Space

God: Be kind and compassionate to one another, forgiving each other, just as in Christ I forgave you (see Ephesians 4:32).

Mom:

_____

_____

_____

_____

_____

_____

_____

_____

God: By one sacrifice I have made perfect forever those who are being made holy (see Hebrews 10:14).

Mom:

_____

_____

_____

_____

_____

_____

_____

_____

Soccer
Momism

"That's enough sugar."

36

GIVE THANKS

Thanksgiving is a traditional American holiday that brings to mind a table decorated in lovely fall colors, bountifully laden with comfort foods like turkey, dressing, mashed potatoes and gravy. Oh yes, and pumpkin pie—don't forget the pie! Such bounty is a stark contrast to the first harvest celebration enjoyed by those founding families so many years ago.

It was in the winter of 1620 when the Pilgrims, traveling by sea from England, settled at Plymouth, Massachusetts. They came seeking religious freedom, with a desire to worship God and to live according to the Holy Scriptures instead of at the whimsy of a pagan king. But the cost was high. The country they met was bleak and uninviting, with several inches of snow already on the ground. Of the 102 passengers aboard the *Mayflower*, nearly half died during the first winter of the "great sickness." After 10 months of hardship and personal tragedy, they gave thanks.

Thanks?

According to settler Edward Winslow, they were grateful to God for His provision in their lives. Winslow wrote in his journal, "And although it be not always so plentiful as it was at this time with us, yet by the goodness of God, we are so far from want that we often wish you partakers of our plenty."

And we do. Every day, we partake in the goodness of our God. Our thankfulness is not dependent on income or health—

as the Pilgrims discovered, those things are temporal. Rather, our thankfulness is rooted in something more lasting—a relationship with the living God. He is the one who reaches out, sustaining us no matter what comes.

So as we gather around the table during the holiday season, let us remember why we too are so far from want. It's because of the goodness of a holy God who saved us. And for those of us who know Him . . . that's plenty.

!!! MOM TALK !!!

How has God sustained you during the difficult times? When was a time you experienced plenty? Take time now to thank God for being there whatever comes your way.

> **Soccer Mom Tip**
> Invite other moms over for a "Teatime Clothing Swap." Everyone brings over her child's outgrown clothes to trade (this works with used books, too).

Lynne's Famous Pumpkin Bread Recipe

Ingredients:

3 ¹/₂ cups flour
2 tsp. baking soda
1 tsp. salt
2 tsp. cinnamon
1 ¹/₂ tsps. nutmeg
1 cup vegetable or olive oil
3 cups sugar
4 eggs
²/₃ cup water
1 large can of pumpkin
1 cup chopped walnuts

Directions: Sift dry ingredients together in a large mixing bowl. Make a "well" and add remaining ingredients. Beat until smooth. Pour into three greased and floured bread loaf pans. Bake at

350°F for 45 to 60 minutes. A toothpick inserted into the center of the loaf should come out clean. Cool slightly in pan, then turn onto cooling racks. Serve. (Also freezes nicely.)

Mom's Space

God: I will supply all your needs according to My riches in glory in Christ Jesus (see Philippians 4:19).

Mom:

_____

_____

_____

_____

_____

God: In times of disaster you will not wither; in days of famine you will enjoy plenty (see Psalm 37:19).

Mom:

_____

_____

_____

_____

_____

_____

A Tough Act to Follow

It has often been said that when something looks easy to do, it only reveals the brilliance of the artist. One day I learned how difficult it is to craft stories like Jesus did, ones that move a heart toward repentance. Of course it was only fitting that my lesson came from a child.

"Mommy, can I have a cookie?" my chubby-fingered little angel asked me.

"No, it's almost time for dinner," I replied.

My daughter knew very well that no means *no* until you can find someone who tells you yes. This is where persistence pays off . . . if you don't get caught.

Daddy is a vulnerable target, especially when The Princess enters the room. My husband inadvertently usurped my authority by okaying the treat, getting snookered by someone not even half his age.

After the deed was discovered, my daughter did penance with a time-out and lost cookie privileges. I should have quit while I was ahead. Instead, I took it on myself to attempt reaching deep into her conscience by telling her a parable (in this case a fable—it involved animals) in order to evoke repentance.

The story went like this: *There was once a little pig that asked her mommy for a piece of candy. The mommy pig said no, so she asked the daddy pig and he said yes, so she got a piece of candy. The next day, she asked the mommy pig to go outside and the mommy pig said no. So she asked the daddy pig and he said yes, and she got to go outside. The following day the little pig felt so bad. Her tummy even ached, because deep inside she knew that she was making a bad choice. Then the little pig prayed for God to forgive her for her bad choices. The End.*

I faced my daughter and went for the big close. "Sweetheart, is there something you'd like to pray about?" I waited, expecting to hear a toddler version of the Sinner's Prayer.

"Yes," she said teary-eyed and concerned. "I'd like to pray for the pig."

Yep! The Lord is the master storyteller. Who could compete with Him?

!!! Mom Talk !!!

What is your child's favorite Bible story? What story from the Bible touches your heart the most? Take a moment to find your favorite story in the Bible and re-read it.

 Soccer Mom Tip
Start a mom co-op. Once a week, one mom takes everyone's kids for three hours. Rotate to the next mom the following week.

Famous Stories Jesus Told

The Wise and the Foolish Builders (Matt. 7:24-27)

The Sower (Matt. 13:3-23; Mark 4:4-20; Luke 8:5-15)

The Tares (Matt. 13:24-30)

The Laborers in the Vineyard (Matt. 20:1-16)

The Talents (Matt. 25:14-30; Luke 19:11-27)

The Good Samaritan (Luke 10:30-37)

The Unmerciful Servant (Matt. 18:23-35)

The Rich Fool (Luke 12:16-21)

The Prodigal Son (Luke 15:11-32)

 Mom's Space

God: My word is living and active. It's sharper than any double-edged sword and penetrates to your very core; it judges the thoughts and attitudes of your heart (see Hebrews 4:12).

Mom:

_____

_____

_____

_____

_____

_____

_____

God: My word is a lamp for your feet and a light for your path so that you know where to go (see Psalm 119:105).

Mom:

_____

_____

_____

_____

_____

_____

_____

38

Soccer
Momism

"Did you have a bad dream?"

LOOKING GOOD

I look into the mirror and sigh. What happened? Where is that young woman with the strawberry-blonde hair and size-three frame? At first I'm left wondering if I've fallen victim to some food preservative gone awry, thrust upon an unsuspecting population. Perhaps I've been afflicted with a yet-to-be discovered disease that expedites the aging process. Or maybe there really is such a thing as an invasion of the body snatchers, because this sure isn't the one I started with. Finally I succumb to the reality that I chose this physical state of disarray.

I decided that having children was worth much more than a lifelong pursuit of youth. I gave up perky breasts for the privilege of nourishing my precious infants. My arms are no longer buff enough to be featured in a body magazine, but they are more than amply sufficient for rocking a sleeping child. My perfect cover-girl skin has given way to the many wrinkles accumulated by late-night vigils over a sick child and worries when a teen comes in late. My thin frame, discarded long ago, has been replaced by a womanly figure that spends more energy trying to cultivate a child's future than hours at the gym, fending off a few extra pounds.

My counselor friend tells me that I need to grieve the loss of my youth. If that means crying over a pint of Ben & Jerry's ice cream, then I guess I've had my funeral.

Glancing back at the mirror, I realize that the young woman I once was is gone forever, replaced by someone with a less-than-perfect body but a much deeper soul.

I think that in God's eyes that makes me pretty glamorous.

!!! Mom Talk !!!

What is your favorite of your physical characteristics? Fill in this blank below.

Example:

I just love <u>Lynne,</u> the woman with <u>the sweet smile.</u>

I just love _____, the woman
(your name)

with _____.
(favorite physical feature)

Now say it out loud to yourself. Praise God for making you precious both inside and out!

Soccer Mom Tip
To limit germ sharing at the doctor's office, bring your own toys and a blanket to spread for your child to sit on.

Rate Your Favorite Ice Cream in Order

_____ Chocolate Mint Chip

_____ Cookies & Cream

_____ Black Walnut

_____ Chocolate Chip Cookie Dough

_____ Rainbow Sherbet

_____ Mocha Almond Fudge

_____ French Vanilla

_____ Pistachio Nut

_____ Rocky Road

_____ Strawberry

_____ Pralines & Cream

_____ Others:

_____

_____

_____

_____

_____

_____

# Mom's Space

God: Charm is deceptive and beauty is fleeting, but a woman who has reverence for Me is to be praised (see Proverbs 31:10).

Mom:

_____

_____

_____

_____

_____

_____

_____

_____

God: Your beauty should come from inside you, the unfading beauty of a gentle and quiet spirit, which is of great worth in My sight (see 1 Peter 3:4).

Mom:

_____

_____

_____

_____

_____

_____

_____

Soccer
Momism
"Be kind."

39

LESSER GODS

One Sunday in March, I was feeding my daughter in her high chair when the phone rang and my life changed. Matthew, my best friend's 16-month-old son, had just drowned in a few inches of water in his backyard.

I couldn't speak for a while, only moan and sob. The rest of the day and the weeks following were surreal: the trip to the hospital where Matthew was pronounced dead, the memorial service, lunch together after the tragedy, our families' camping trip a few months later.

Throughout that season, I searched for meaning and tried to make sense out of what I believed to be senseless. When I finally tried to summarize my feelings, I was surprised to find I felt betrayed by God. I believed God was my best friend, yet I felt like He had stabbed me in the back. How could He allow this to happen to such good people—*His* people? Who was this God whom I worshiped each Sunday, prayed to and visited with all week long?

Then God whispered ever so softly, "It's not Me."

In time, I learned that I had been worshiping the wrong god, inventing attributes that the true God never embodied. He is neither an apathetic god nor a god who does things my way. Time spent in Scripture eventually helped me recognize and refute those false beliefs.

Today as I face life's sorrows, I do so with the God whose ways are not my own, whose mission it is to love and comfort me, who calls me to join Him in His best, who has enough power to make positive changes in my life, and who will never leave me, no matter what comes. He has promised me these things.

He is, as the apostle Thomas proclaimed, "My Lord and my God!" (John 20:28). To worship any other is futile.

!!! Mom Talk !!!

Have you had difficulty accepting something that God has allowed? What beliefs do you have about God that are inconsistent with the Bible? Talk with God about your concerns and give yourself permission to grieve while God comforts you.

> **Soccer Mom Tip**
>
> Are your kids screaming in the back seat? Don't compromise your safety by turning around to discipline. Find the nearest parking lot, pull in, and tell them the car doesn't move until it's quiet.

Are You Trusting Any False Gods?

False god	True God
The god who changes.	"Jesus Christ is the same yesterday, today, and forever" (Hebrews 13:8).
The god who is impotent.	"You can do all things; no plan of yours can be thwarted" (Job 42:2).
The god who is apathetic.	"The LORD . . . will never let the righteous fall" (Psalm 55:22).
The god who is harsh.	"The Father of compassion and . . . all comfort" (2 Corinthians 1:3).
The god who does things my way.	"Neither are your ways my ways declares the Lord" (Isaiah 55:8).

Mom's Space

God: Turn to Me and be saved, all you ends of the earth; for I am God, and there is no other (Isaiah 45:22).

Mom:

_____

_____

_____

_____

_____

_____

_____

_____

God: Find rest for your soul in Me alone; your hope comes from Me (see Psalm 62:5).

Mom:

_____

_____

_____

_____

_____

_____

_____

_____

TINY DANCER

When my daughter told me that she wanted to quit ballet, I cried. How could she so easily give up the natural ability to move as graceful as a feather floating on a spring breeze? Of course I didn't want to make it about me (well, it was a *little* bit about me), so I begged and pleaded as subtly as I could. It didn't work. My daughter informed me that she had watched the older kids dance, and after talking with them, had found out about the rigorous practice schedule that would be required when performing at that level. She discovered there were things they had to give up, like time spent with friends or after-school activities. She informed me that she wasn't willing to commit to that. Leave it to my 10-year-old to count the cost. Then I remembered that Jesus asked His disciples to do the same:

> Suppose one of you wants to build a tower. Will he not first sit down and estimate the cost to see if he has enough money to complete it? . . . In the same way, any of you who does not give up everything he has cannot be my disciple (Luke 14:28,33).

Wow. That's hard to hear. Living a life totally devoted to God isn't easy. Not only do I have to give up retaliating against a person who has wronged me, but I also have to actually love her! It's not enough to stay faithful to my husband by avoiding adultery; I'm supposed to remain loyal in my thoughts as well. It's not just about avoiding sinful acts, but it's also about doing good deeds. Most importantly, it's about dying to my flesh and letting the Holy Spirit dictate my daily choices.

I praised my daughter for thinking ahead. If she wasn't willing to sacrifice in order to pursue her goal of prima ballerina, I understood. When it came time to deciding about whether or not to follow our Lord, my daughter and I weighed the cost. We both decided to put on our shoes and dance!

!!! Mom Talk !!!

What have you had to leave behind in order to follow Jesus? What things in your life are keeping you from reaching your spiritual goals? Where do you feel God's Spirit is leading you right now?

> **Soccer Mom Tip**
> Place dishes in a cupboard down low so that your child can unload the dishwasher and put them away within reach.

Ballet Positions

First Position or *Première* (prehm-YAHR)
In this position, the heels and knees are together, with legs turned out from the hips and toes pointed out so that the feet make a V-shape. The arms are out and in front of the torso, forming a soft curve. The spine is straight, and the head, back and pelvis are aligned.

Second Position or *Seconde* (se-GOHND)

In this position, the legs are again turned out from the hips, but the feet are separated about shoulder-width apart, still in a V-shape. Eventually, with practice, the feet may form a straight line. The arms are out to the sides and slightly rounded.

Third Position or *Troisième* (trwah-ZYEM)

Keeping the legs turned out from the hips, the dancer crosses the front heel about halfway in front of the other foot, touching it at the middle. Either foot can be used. If the right foot is in front, the right arm is raised overhead in a semicircle. The left arm is extended out to the side. If the left foot is in front, then the left arm is overhead and the right arm extended.

Fourth Position or *Quatrième* (kah-tree-EHM)

With the legs still turned out from the hips, one foot is placed directly in front of the other, with the forward heel directly in front of the toe of the other foot. There is a space of about 12 inches between the feet. If the right foot is in front, the right arm is raised overhead in a semicircle.

Fifth Position or *Cinquième* (san-KYEM)

With the legs turned out from the hips, the heel of the front foot is placed against the first joint of the other big toe. The arms are lifted and extended overhead into a soft circular shape.

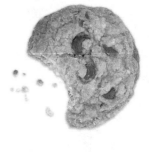

Mom's Space

God: Love Me with all of your heart, with all your soul and with all your strength (see Deuteronomy 6:5).

Mom:

_____

_____

_____

_____

_____

_____

_____

_____

God: You are receiving the goal of your faith, the salvation of your souls (see 1 Peter 1:9).

Mom:

_____

_____

_____

_____

_____

_____

_____

_____

A Job Day

The week started with a bang. On Monday, what we foolishly believed in the wee morning hours was a summer rain turned out to be a broken pipe flooding our flowerbed. Later in the week, our freezer went on the blink, almost robbing us of our hefty Costco investment. After a four-mile ride on Saturday, my mountain bike literally disintegrated, derailer and all. And finally, the *pièce de résistance*: toasted Sienna.

We were on our way to church Sunday morning when we noticed smoke coming from the hood of our Toyota Sienna. My quick-thinking husband pulled out of the busy intersection and got everyone and everything out of the car faster than you could say "Fire drill." As we all stood a safe distance away waiting for the fire truck, I looked over at my husband and smiled. We had survived a week of spiritual boot camp.

Ironically, I was teaching a Sunday School lesson that morning titled "Life Is Not Fair," highlighting the trials of the biblical character Job. Even though I poured several hours and a great deal of prayer into the study, God must have thought I could use a little hands-on experience.

In the Bible, Job didn't like how things were going for him, either. He demanded an explanation from God for why things were so bad. Wow, talk about nerve! Eventually Job had to repent for telling God what to do. When Job came to the conclusion that God knew a whole lot more than he did, he realized bossing God was not really an option after all.

As I reflected back on my week in light of Job's many trials, I decided I'd fared pretty well. I was more than happy to let God be in charge.

!!! MOM TALK !!!

What does a "Job Day" look like for you? Who do you know right now in need of some encouragement? Make a list of the things God has created that are amazing to you.

Soccer Mom Tip

Place a large box or basket at the front door for your kids to drop their shoes in before entering the house, or purchase a box of non-skid hospital shoe covers at your medical supply store to go over dirty shoes.

Soccer Mom Vehicle Emergency Kit

- ❏ Phonebook
- ❏ Flashlight
- ❏ Picnic blanket
- ❏ Extra diaper and wipes
- ❏ Suntan lotion
- ❏ Children's book
- ❏ Extra pair of underwear
- ❏ Roll of paper towels
- ❏ Sealed water bottles
- ❏ Band-Aids
- ❏ Pair of flip-flops
- ❏ Paper cups
- ❏ Granola bars
- ❏ Change of clothes for each child
- ❏ Quarters
- ❏ Children's Liquid Motrin
- ❏ Ball and jump rope

Mom's Space

God: Give thanks in all circumstances, for this is My will for you in Christ Jesus (see 1 Thessalonians 5:18).

Mom:

God: I know how to rescue godly people from trials and to hold the unrighteous for the day of judgment, while continuing their punishment (see 2 Peter 2:9).

Mom:

CONFIDENCE

It was lurking in the garage. The height of the creature struck fear into the heart of our six-year-old son. He stayed as far away as possible from the blue beast, crouching between the lawnmower and the tool chest. It was . . . his bicycle.

Although my son had formerly loved his sweet ride, which was adorned with the coolest of cartoon stickers, its quad status had been diminished by the removal of training wheels. It was transformed, ramp-ready and *terrifying!* We knew he didn't need the extra support, as both trainers were bent upward so badly that neither one actually touched the ground. Yet we surrendered and put them back on, realizing that the security of those wheels gave my son the confidence necessary to mount the mighty aluminum hog and venture into the neighborhood.

I laughed at first; we used to call his add-on equipment a decorator item. But then I remembered my first real job. I'd been educated for the position, studying several years to secure a degree . . . yet I was afraid. *What if I make a mistake? What if they laugh at me? What if I fail?* I turned to my best friend for encouragement: God.

He reminded me that I could do all things through Him who gave me the strength. He told me to keep my eyes on Him and not look down. Best of all He said He'd go with me and hold me up. Thinking back to that time, I remembered what it felt like to desperately need training wheels.

I let my son leave the extra wheels on his bike as long as he wanted; eventually he asked us to remove them. But I've decided to keep *my* training wheels on. I'm smart enough to know that I'll never grow out of my need for the support of a loving God.

!!! MOM TALK !!!

Describe a time in your life when you needed God to be your training wheels as you ventured into something new. In what areas of your life right now do you need God to assist you? People are sometimes training wheels, too. Who do you know that might need you to come alongside her as training wheels?

 Soccer Mom Tip
The night before church, have everyone lay out clothing for the next day. Pack the diaper bag and place it in the car. This will help you get out the door faster.

Garage Scavenger Hunt

Here's what's in my garage. See if you can match my score.

Unused exercise equipment	20 points
Kite (no string)	10 points
Bike with flat tire	20 points
Christmas tree	25 points (10 extra points if the lights are still strung)
Flag	10 points
Extra rolls of toilet paper	5 points for each roll
Drum set	50 points

Paint can	10 points each can (5 extra points if you have no idea which room it's for)
Larryboy helmet	50 points
Bag of clothes (for charity)	25 points for each bag
Empty cage for small animal	20 points
Posters of classic cars	10 points for each poster
Marshmallow gun	25 points
Folding chairs	20 points each chair
Wicker basket	10 points
Fish food (we have no fish)	10 points
Old sneakers	10 points
Fishing poles	20 points each one
Clothing iron (yeah, like I ever use that!)	10 points
Ironing board (ditto above)	10 points
Roller blades	15 points
Skateboard	10 points
Crutches	25 points
Stadium seat cushions	10 points each
Sleeping bags	10 points each
Camp stove	20 points
Lawn mower	15 points
Bag of briquettes	10 points

Score

0 to 100 points: You may want to find a safe place for the key to your storage unit—you're obviously not storing things in your garage.

101 to 400 points: Don't forget to hit the garage sales this weekend—there's still room for more!

Over 400 points: You might want to get an alarm system for your car—we know it isn't in your garage.

Mom's Space

God: Be confident of this, that I who began a good work in you will carry it on to completion until the day of Christ Jesus (see Philippians 1:6).

Mom:

_____

_____

_____

_____

_____

_____

_____

_____

God: Even to your old age and gray hairs I am He who will sustain you. I have made you and I will carry you; I will sustain you and I will rescue you (see Isaiah 46:4).

Mom:

_____

_____

_____

_____

_____

_____

_____

DADDY'S GIRL

I wanted him to always be there for me. I wanted him to spoil me yet discipline me in love. I wanted him to believe the best about me and then make the best happen in my life. I wanted him to impart to me the advice of an ancient sage. I wanted him to be perfect, but he couldn't be . . . he was only a dad.

I was often frustrated with my earthly father for not measuring up to my perfect standard of what a dad should be. I wanted a Superdad; I got an Okaydad. He did his best as all dads try to do, but for me that wasn't enough. I yearned for more.

At the age of 13, I found the Dad I had longed for . . . God. He was more perfect than I had hoped, more Dad than I could've ever dreamed up. He was the Dad any daughter would desire.

When I stopped wanting my dad to be what only God could be, my attitude changed. I realized my earthly father was painfully human, just like me. He was someone in need of a healing touch, just like me. He was imperfect, just like me.

Now as a parent myself, I realize that I wouldn't want my children to compare me to God; I'd fall short. Really, there is only One who will never disappoint. So I've decided to introduce my children to their heavenly Father very early, before they start demanding something from me that I was never created to deliver.

!!! Mom Talk !!!

In what ways do you lack as a parent? What are the things you may need to forgive your earthly father for? What do you value most about your heavenly Father?

Soccer Mom Tip

Always double the recipe when you make lasagna, enchiladas or casseroles. Freeze the extra for a no-stress dinner later in the month.

10 Fun Ways for Dad to Spend Quality Time with His Daughter

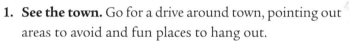

1. **See the town.** Go for a drive around town, pointing out areas to avoid and fun places to hang out.
2. **Dine out.** Eat at a restaurant that doesn't serve toys in a bag. Make it a fancy night out.
3. **Drink mochas.** Visit your local coffeehouse/bookstore.
4. **Get fit.** Go bike riding, rollerblading or scootering.
5. **Take in a movie.** Ice cream afterward is a must.
6. **See the game.** Go to a professional or semi-professional sports activity.
7. **Share a hobby.** Collect stamps, paint or build something together.
8. **Play games.** Go bowling, golfing or hit the arcades.
9. **Shop.** This may be the only chance you have at helping her pick out an outfit. It also provides a great opportunity for a healthy talk about modesty.
10. **Take a risk.** Ask her what she wants to do. After all, you'll expect her potential dates to think of her needs.

Mom's Space

God: Your father disciplined you for a little while as he thought best; but I discipline you for your good, that you may share in My holiness (see Hebrews 12:10).

Mom:

_____

_____

_____

_____

_____

_____

_____

God: I will open my hand and satisfy the desires of every living thing (see Psalm 145:16).

Mom:

_____

_____

_____

_____

_____

_____

_____

SOWING

I won an argument today. Two days ago, my daughter wanted to make a skirt, and of course I ran to the local fabric store. I am totally inept at sewing, so I relied on the clerk at the counter to help me purchase the correct amount of material, including trim. I paid for my purchase and went home. Two days later, Cassie discovered a problem: The clerk hadn't cut enough trim . . . it was four inches too short.

I was very frustrated. Shouldn't a person at a fabric store know how to read a pattern? I marched over to the store, only to discover that they don't carry that type of trim anymore. Two days later. Now I was mad.

I told the store manager to make sure that in the future all of her employees are trained to correctly read pattern requirements. I huffed and left. I was right . . . and very wrong. If I filled out a job application to be hired as judge and jury over everyone who makes a mistake, I would be hired on the spot. Unfortunately, that's not my career goal.

Instead, I have applied for another job description. It is to be a living, breathing sacrifice, to serve others and administer the kind of grace my Lord has bestowed upon me. I'm to die to self and think of other's needs before my own. Today I would have been in the unemployment line.

As Bible Answer Man Dr. Walter Martin used to say, "It doesn't matter if you win the battle but lose the soul." In the scheme of things, I'm almost positive that souls cost more than the price of trim.

!!! Mom Talk !!!

When was the last time you got frustrated by someone's mistake? When was the last time you messed up or disappointed someone? Think of someone you may have wounded with your words. Consider going back to apologize for forgetting to offer grace.

Soccer Mom Tip

Place written labels on objects in the house, such as "window," "door" and "chair," in order to encourage reading skills.

Sewing Definitions

Basting: Temporarily joining fabric together with large removable stitches for the purpose of testing the fit.

Seam allowance: The area between the stitching and raw, cut edge of the fabric.

Facing: Area of the garment that is turned to the inside rather than having an exposed raw edge of fabric.

Interfacing: A part of the outfit you don't see that adds body to the fabric.

Remnants: Small discounted pieces of fabric.

Under-stitching: A stitch by hand or machine that assists a facing or lining to stay unseen and not roll.

Hem: The bottom edge that is turned under on a garment.

 # Mom's Space

God: Pursue righteousness, godliness, faith, love, endurance and gentleness (see 1 Timothy 6:11).

Mom:

_____

_____

_____

_____

_____

_____

_____

_____

God: Do nothing out of selfish ambition or vain conceit, but in humility consider others better than yourself (see Philippians 2:3).

Mom:

_____

_____

_____

_____

_____

_____

_____

_____

Soccer
Momism
"Would you like a snack?"

LAUGH

I used to be fun. As a college girl I played my fair share of jokes on many of my friends. It was me who answered the door in green face cream and rollers to freak my guy friend out. I distinctly remember the night we cookie-and-whipped-creamed my boyfriend's car. Then there was the night 10 of us girls crammed ourselves into the boys' bathroom stall at a ritzy restaurant for photos. I remember when my girlfriend and I cranked up the stereo, pulled the car over and danced on the side of the road to our latest music crush.

Now I'm not so fun anymore. I get on my children about their homework and chores. I try to pay all of my bills and drive everyone to their appointments on time. I fix dinner and clean—a lot. I break up sibling squabbles and ground disobedient children. I get tired. I miss the fun me.

Jesus was fun. He attended weddings like the one at Cana, went to dinners at people's homes, and enjoyed Holy Day feasts and celebrations. Jesus must have understood the delicate balance between duty and the refreshment of one's soul. As it says in the book of Ecclesiastes, "There is a time for everything, and a season for every activity under heaven."

I've decided that life is too short to go through it without joy, too difficult not to take time to laugh. Today before my kids get home from school, I'm digging toward the back of my closet to find that fun girl of yesterday. I'm going to invite her over for the afternoon. I think my kids will like her a lot.

Now where did I put that silly string?

!!! MOM TALK !!!

What kind of crazy and fun things did you do as a teen? What fun thing can you do to bring laughter into your family's day?

 Soccer Mom Tip
Have your teen make a list of the qualities he or she wants in a spouse someday. Then when Mister or Miss Wonderful appears, compare that person to the list to see if the "crush" measures up to the teen's standards.

Crazy Mama: Silly Things to Do with Your Kids

- Dress up as clowns and take pictures of each other.
- Purposely sing out of tune.
- Greet your teen with a can of silly string when he or she gets home.
- Do a role switch. Act the part of child while your child gets to play parent.
- Serve dessert first at the evening meal.
- Have a goofy dance contest.
- Serve a birthday cake for dessert when it's no one's birthday. Be sure to sing "Happy Birthday to no one!"
- Stop the car in an empty parking lot, kill the engine, and have everyone run around the vehicle three times and jump back in.

Mom's Space

God: May the righteous be glad and rejoice before Me; may they be happy and joyful (see Psalm 68:31).

Mom:

_____

_____

_____

_____

_____

_____

_____

_____

_____

God: You are clothed with strength and dignity; you can laugh at the days to come (see Proverbs 31:25).

Mom:

_____

_____

_____

_____

_____

_____

_____

Soccer
Momism
"You're so creative!"

SAY IT AGAIN

They say I had 20 babies that day. It's kind of strange—I don't
remember having even one.

My husband and I learned just two weeks before the due
date of our first child that this baby had inherited one of my
most bothersome character traits: a poor sense of direction.
The baby was breech and too large to turn, so a C-section was
scheduled. The day before surgery, I cleaned house and finished
"nesting" in preparation for the big event. Last on my to-do list
was a quick trip to the grocery store. Jumping into the truck,
I paused and prayed, "God, please protect me and this precious
little one inside. Amen."

Two blocks from home I attempted a left turn and was hit
by another vehicle traveling way too fast. My truck spun like a
top several times and ended up on a nearby lawn. Witnesses say
that I got out of the truck woozy and bloodied from a gash in
the back of my head, mechanically recited information about
who to contact, then lost consciousness.

A thorough examination revealed that I was out of danger
but had suffered a concussion. When I regained consciousness, my short-term memory was impaired. I asked the same

questions over and over, unable to retain the answers. My husband wrote down the answers on a piece of paper. When I began my barrage of questions, he'd simply reply, "Refer to the sheet of paper in front of you." I would read it with surprise, pause and begin the entire process all over again. This continued for 11 hours.

"It's a girl!" the doctor announced. Yet due to my memory loss, I couldn't remember what he said. Every few minutes he re-announced the sex of my baby, and over and over I responded with first-time exuberance.

Later that evening, the nurse came and placed our beautiful healthy girl into my arms. All at once, my memory started to return. I experienced an overwhelming sense that this little person and I had been through something pretty traumatic and that God had honored my prayer and had protected us.

Today I still do not remember the car accident or the birth of my daughter, but I will never forget how fortunate we were . . . and I don't need my husband to write that one down.

!!! MOM TALK !!!

Can you remember a time when God intervened to protect you or someone you loved? Take this time to write down a list of the many things you are currently thankful for.

 ### Soccer Mom Tip

Keep a toddler toy drawer in the kitchen for times when you need to prepare a meal and keep an eye on your little one at the same time. Make sure it's safely away from kitchen hazards like the stove.

Popular Boys' Baby Names

Nationality	Name	Meaning
American	Jacob	he grasps the heel
Egyptian	Rameses	born of the sun
Israeli	Aaron	exalted
Spanish	Alejandro	defends mankind
Romanian	Radu	happy
Chinese	Gan	adventure
African	Abayomi	brings happiness
Portuguese	Celio	heaven
Irish	Seafra	peace from God

Popular Girls' Baby Names

Nationality	Name	Meaning
American	Emily	industrious
Egyptian	Nashwa	wonderful feeling
Israeli	Abaigeal	gives joy
Spanish	Adalia	nobility
Romanian	Mihaela	who is like God
Chinese	Mei zhen	beautiful pearl
African	Alika	most beautiful
Portuguese	Emiliana	rival
Irish	Teagan	good-looking

Mom's Space

God: Devote yourselves to prayer, being watchful and thankful (see Colossians 4:2).

Mom:

_____

_____

_____

_____

_____

_____

_____

_____

_____

God: Many are the wonders I have done. The things I planned for you no one can recount—there would be too many to declare (see Psalm 40:5).

Mom:

_____

_____

_____

_____

_____

_____

_____

_____

Soccer
Momism
*"Open up . . . here
comes the airplane."*

47

THE TRUMP

When it's time for my son to come home from the neighbor-hood park, I call him in. No, I don't use a cell phone. Giving a cell phone to my 10-year-old would turn a *Go* phone into a *Gone* phone. I don't scamper around the park calling him either . . . why would he answer me? There's no benefit on his part—answering me would mean he'd have to leave.

I call him in by circling the park in my van while honking my horn at 10-second intervals. Everyone knows my van. And they know why I'm honking. Peer pressure wins out as people stare at my son as if to say, "Make her stop!" So he comes running. Lately, my honking calls are commanding a quicker response. I think I'm down to five beeps.

The other day I was reflecting on the strange way I collect my child. But then I remembered that my Lord has adopted a similar retrieval system. There will come a day very soon when this world will have run its course. The wars will end, hedonism will die and sorrows will cease. In 1 Corinthians 15, my Lord says that "the trumpet will sound, the dead will be raised imperishable, and we will be changed" (v. 52). When that happens, death will forever lose its sting, sin will be swallowed up in the victory won on our behalf through Jesus Christ and I will put on a new body of immortality.

I don't know about you, but I'm listening very closely for that horn, and then I'll come running.

!!! Mom Talk !!!

How do you call your child in from play? Imagine what your favorite part of heaven will be like. What is something about this world that you won't miss?

> ### Soccer Mom Tip
> If your toddler pitches a fit in the middle of grocery shopping, ask a clerk to push your cart into cold storage until you get back. Then go to the car with your child to regroup before retuning to finish your shopping.

More Bible Trumpets

Joel 2:1: "Blow the **trumpet** in Zion; sound the alarm on my holy hill. Let all who live in the land tremble, for the day of the LORD is coming. It is close at hand."

Matthew 24:31: "And he will send his angels with a loud **trumpet** call, and they will gather his elect from the four winds, from one end of the heavens to the other."

1 Thessalonians 4:16: "For the Lord himself will come down from heaven, with a loud command, with the voice of the archangel and with the **trumpet** call of God, and the dead in Christ will rise first."

Revelation 1:10: "On the Lord's Day I was in the Spirit, and I heard behind me a loud voice like a **trumpet**."

Mom's Space

God: Through faith you are shielded by My power until the coming of the salvation that is ready to be revealed in the last time (see 1 Peter 1:5).

Mom:

God: You are not in darkness so that this day should surprise you like a thief (see 1 Thessalonians 5:4).

Mom:

48

EMBRACE

Amidst the chaos of one of my more exasperating days, I took a trip into the future. Kind of a mommy wormhole. Things were just as I expected. My house was clean. No more food stuck between couch cushions, no more candy wrappers in the corner of the bedroom. The bathroom smelled linen-fresh. There was a full roll of toilet paper on the spindle. The toothpaste was capped and in the drawer, and there were no fingerprints on the mirror. The refrigerator was full, and the milk was sitting upright. So was the soda pop. The laundry was washed and folded. Every shirt and pair of pants hung perfectly ironed in the closet, organized by color.

My car had a full tank of gas. It smelled like a car, not like a fast-food restaurant serving wet socks. It was quiet when I drove and no one was arguing in the seat behind me. I knew where my cell phone was, and I wasn't over on minutes. I made it to all of my appointments on time. My husband and I rendezvoused for a romantic dinner.

When we returned home from dinner in my future life, the house was very quiet. I didn't have anyone to help with homework. There were no teenage dramas to hear about, no one wanting to go to the park. I fixed a snack that no one ate. Because all the chores were finished, I read a book . . . to myself. Suddenly I am wet.

Wet?!

"Sorry, Mom, I didn't mean to spill my drink. I'll get a paper towel."

I've been transported back into the present. The television is turned up loud in order to compete with the blaring stereo coming from the back room. The phone rings at the same time as the doorbell. A group of boys with a football ask if they can hang out and play video games in the back room with my son. My husband walks in the front door carrying pizza, complaining that someone forgot to mow the lawn. The teacher on the phone wants to discuss my child's missing math assignments at school. My daughter, reeking of nail polish, frantically wipes up the mess. And I am still wet. Not from a spilled drink, but from tears.

I am home.

!!! Mom Talk !!!

What drives you crazy right now that you will probably miss when your children leave? What drives your children crazy about you that they will laugh about later? Dream about the exciting things God may want you to do after your children leave home.

 Soccer Mom Tip
Give your child tokens and a TV guide to select shows and purchase television time for the week. When the tokens are gone, their TV for the week is done. This also works for electronic games.

When the Children Leave, Dream Big!

- Take a college course or pursue a degree.

- Sell your house, downsize and go live in a foreign country for a year.

- Offer your home as a weekend getaway for pastors and wives.

- Train for a marathon.

- Start a ministry for young moms.

- Sponsor a child overseas and visit him or her.

- Take a short-term missions trip.

- Volunteer at the local homeless shelter or crisis pregnancy center.

- Learn to play an instrument or take vocal lessons.

- Write a book or family memoir.

- Tutor children in reading at the neighborhood school.

- Develop a website or blog highlighting your interests.

- Start a prayer group of empty nesters and together ask God, "What's next?"

Mom's Space

God: Keep an eye on everyone in your household, and keep them all busy and productive (see Proverbs 31:27).

Mom:

_____

_____

_____

_____

_____

_____

_____

God: There is a time for everything, and a season for every activity under heaven (see Ecclesiastes 3:1).

Mom:

_____

_____

_____

_____

_____

_____

_____

_____

YOU ARE KNOWN

I didn't want to go to the women's church retreat. I'd heard
they were going to do crafts. I hate crafts. I don't have the col-
oring gene, or the sewing gene, or the cooking . . . well, you
get the idea. Besides, I had heard everyone cries at these kinds
of gatherings, and I didn't want to cry. Crying means you lose
control, and I am the Queen Bee of Control.

Yet, try as I may, I was unable to come up with an adequate
excuse not to go. My husband would watch the kids, my girlfriend Jenni wanted to drive, and I had finished all of my work
assignments. So off I went.

On the way to the conference, my friend and I decided to
take a little excursion. The tiny mountain town we stopped in
offered an array of specialty shops, my favorites of which featured various kinds of teapots. For the past month I had been
in hot pursuit of a white and blue teapot, but I was so picky
that I hadn't found the perfect one. This time was no different.
I dragged my poor friend from shop to shop examining every
kind of pot, but none met up to my ideal standard.

After finally making it to the conference, I sat alone in my
room while my friend headed out to breakfast. I don't do breakfast. I figured I'd hide out in my little room, read Scripture and
pray. I had started to question God and figured this was the best

time to sort things out. Did He really have His hand on me? Count the hairs on my head? Did He really know me by name? I decided to ask God directly.

"Okay, God, I'm here."

Just as I thought, silence. I spoke a bit louder in case He was busy or something.

"Hello? Do You even know I'm here?"

Nothing. Maybe I should have stayed home after all.

My quiet time was turning out to be a bust and my stomach had decided it was hungry after all, so I trekked over to breakfast. I plopped down next to Jenni just in time for the morning door prize. And as luck would have it, my name was drawn.

I trudged over to the prize table laden with wrapped gifts of various shapes and sizes. I grabbed one and sat down. "Open it, open it!" my friend insisted. I peeled off the paper and lifted the lid on the box. Jenni gasped. "No way!" I held up one of the three candles, all molded in the shape of white and blue teapots.

God knew I was here, and I cried.

!!! MOM TALK !!!

When do you feel out of control? What does God know about you that others may not? How has God let you know that He is right here with you?

⚽ Soccer Mom Tip

Encourage personal responsibility. Buy your child an alarm clock and set it to get up for school the next day. If he is late, set up a consequence, such as make-up time at school.

Lynne's Friendship-Scone Recipe

Ingredients:
2 cups flour
1 $\frac{1}{4}$ tbs. baking powder
3 tbs. sugar
$\frac{1}{2}$ tsp. salt
$\frac{1}{2}$ cup ground walnuts
1 tsp. vanilla
6 tbs. butter (not margarine)
$\frac{1}{2}$ cup + 1 tbs. milk or buttermilk

Directions: Preheat oven to 425°F. Mix dry ingredients together and then cut in butter. Add vanilla and milk. Do not overmix. Turn out onto floured surface and roll into a 6- to 8-inch round about 2 inches thick. Cut into pie wedges and place on greased baking sheet. Bake 10 to 20 minutes or until light brown.

Cream to Serve with Scones
Mix a small carton of heavy whipping cream with $\frac{1}{2}$ cube of cream cheese on medium to high speed until formed peaks are firm. Add powdered sugar to taste. Serve alongside your favorite jam.

# Mom's Space

God: Every good and perfect gift is from above, coming down from Me, the Father of the heavenly lights. I do not change like shifting shadows (see James 1:7).

Mom:

_____

_____

_____

_____

_____

_____

_____

God: Now you see but a poor reflection as in a mirror; then you shall see face to face. Now you know in part; then you shall know fully, even as I fully know you (see 1 Corinthians 13:12).

Mom:

_____

_____

_____

_____

_____

_____

_____

Soccer
Momism
"Wear your helmet!"

FRIENDSHIP WARFARE

She is my polar opposite. Perhaps that is why our friendship started off with a bang. I am expressive and opinionated; she is more stoic and reserved. I appreciate her ability to complete tasks; she admires my love for people. I am hyper; she is calm. I'm right-handed; she's a lefty. She's country; and I'm, well, a little bit rock 'n' roll.

The intimacy that developed between Heidi and me was amazing. We quickly grew into soul mates. Our friendship was a model that others admired and some even envied. We went just about everywhere together, from shopping and lunches out to family camping and church socials. I was her Lamaze coach; she held my hand during my husband's surgery. Then something went wrong.

Heidi stopped calling as often. At first, I just figured she was busy. Then she didn't return my calls. Again, I chalked it up to a busy life; after all, she had a husband and three children. Then she began canceling all our social appointments, yet she still had time for other friends. I started sensing that she was pulling away from the relationship. I spent several sleepless nights trying to figure out what I did wrong. Was it something I'd said? Something I didn't say?

I eventually discovered that Heidi and I had a different opinion about friendship. Heidi's idea of friendship was for me to respect her privacy. She desired to reveal herself at her own pace: slowly, cautiously. She had emotionally disclosed more of herself than she felt comfortable with, just to keep up. Unfortunately, she lacked the boundary words to shout "Slow down!" She had set hidden land mines instead of boundaries, and my "tank" had charged right over most of them. She felt violated; I felt rejected and betrayed.

Cindi, another friend of mine, explained that there are levels of intimacy in every friendship. Level I relationships are based on common interests. Level IIs are based on one person's needs and the other person's attempts to meet those needs. In Level III relationships, both parties are able to fully and safely disclose who they really are to each other. Not everyone is ready for a Level III experience. For some, it takes years to build the trust that is necessary for the friendship to mature.

There are lessons I've gleaned from my experience with Heidi, mistakes I won't repeat. I now keep my tank in first gear, and realize that my ability to become intimate fast can be a blessing to some and a curse to others who aren't quite ready to delve into a close friendship. I've also learned that there is someone who always desires a Level III relationship with me— my best friend, Jesus.

!!! MOM TALK !!!

What is your expectation of friendship? When have you been disappointed in friendships? How would you define your friendship with God?

Soccer Mom Tip

Give your teen a certain amount of money to spend on toiletries, such as shampoo, toothpaste, hairspray and soap. Then make Mom and Dad's supplies off-limits.

What Level Are You?

Communication is vital to the survival of any friendship. Ask your friend the following questions before a battle ensues:

- How are we different?

- What is your definition of a close friend?

- What topics have made you feel uncomfortable?

- Can we have a code word that means "I need my space"?

- What do you enjoy most about our friendship?

- Are you content with the way that our friendship is progressing?

- Do you feel a need to limit the time we spend together?

- Do you want my opinion on this topic, or would you like me to listen quietly?

Mom's Space

God: A person with many companions may come to ruin, but there is a friend who sticks closer than a brother (see Proverbs 18:24).

Mom:

_____

God: For great is My love toward you, and My faithfulness endures forever (see Psalm 117:2).

Mom:

_____

THE GOAL

My friend Pauline told me that when she was a young mother, she could hardly wait for her kids to leave home so that she could start her ministry. Then one day she realized . . . *they* were her ministry. And that's exactly the way it is. We moms may not be currently running a homeless shelter, traveling to Africa to battle AIDS, or lobbying on behalf of religious issues, but we are in ministry fulltime.

Potty training, playgroups, homework and extra-curricular events are the nuts and bolts of what we do. Hidden in all of those activities are opportunities to build character in those who have been placed in our charge. We teach love, joy, peace, patience, kindness, goodness, faithfulness, gentleness and self-control. The fruits of our labor will carry our precious children forward into the ministry our Lord has created especially for them. Oh, sometimes it gets loud and looks a bit messy, but there is real work going on. Ministry doesn't always look how we think it should, but it was pretty messy for Jesus, too.

When I think of God going into ministry, I picture a president giving out detailed directives to his advisory board. There would be an overabundance of financial assets due to perfectly written donor letters. Of course no one would die in the field because with God nothing like that happens. I imagine a ministry led with authority and pure unmitigated power, forcing people to conversion.

But that's not the way it was with Jesus. When an all-powerful God made plans to save the world from itself, it looked very humble. It looked human.

We read in the book of Philippians that Jesus "being the very nature of God did not consider equality with God something to be grasped; but made himself nothing, taking the very nature of a servant, being made in human likeness. And being found in the appearance as a man, he humbled himself and became obedient to death—even death on a cross" (2:6-8).

A *servant*. Now there's a role we moms can relate to. In my servant role as a sports mom, ballet mom, music mom, paintball mom, drama mom, church mom or just plain mom, I want to model the example of ministry set by my Lord, who gave Himself freely, lovingly and without holding back. Then I will someday be able to boast that I did not do all this in vain. That every runny nose wiped, bad attitude corrected and laundry load folded was for a purpose. Then someday soon I will finish the race set before me. I will have kept the faith. I will have netted the goal.

PUZZLE SOLUTIONS

Soccer Mom Sudoku (pages 26-27)

#1

2	5	9	1	8	3	6	4	7
4	7	3	2	5	6	8	1	9
8	6	1	7	4	9	3	5	2
1	3	8	4	7	5	9	2	6
9	4	7	6	1	2	5	8	3
6	2	5	9	3	8	4	7	1
5	8	2	3	9	7	1	6	4
7	9	4	5	6	1	2	3	8
3	1	6	8	2	4	7	9	5

#2

1	8	7	2	3	6	5	9	4
2	5	9	8	1	4	3	7	6
3	6	4	7	5	9	1	2	8
9	4	6	3	2	5	8	1	7
5	3	1	9	7	8	6	4	2
7	2	8	6	4	1	9	3	5
6	1	5	4	9	7	2	8	3
8	7	3	1	6	2	4	5	9
4	9	2	5	8	3	7	6	1

Word Bee (page 39)

(1) disagree–oppose; (2) beginning–commencement; (3) discipline–restraint; (4) harmony–agreement; (5) celebration–party; (6) children–offspring; (7) curious–inquisitive; (8) sleepy–lethargic; (9) joy–elation; (10) thankful–appreciative

Match the Currency with the Country (page 42)

United States–dollar; South Korea–won; Mexico–peso; Japan–yen; India–rupee; Israel–shekel; Italy–euro; Niger–franc; Uganda–shilling; Egypt–pound

Capital Challenge! (page 69)

Alabama–Montgomery; Alaska–Juneau; Arizona–Phoenix; Arkansas–Little Rock; California–Sacramento; Colorado–Denver; Connecticut–Hartford; Delaware–Dover; Florida–Tallahassee; Georgia–Atlanta; Hawaii–Honolulu; Idaho–Boise; Illinois–Springfield; Indiana–Indianapolis; Iowa–Des Moines; Kansas–Topeka; Kentucky–Frankfort; Louisiana–Baton Rouge; Maine–Augusta; Maryland–Annapolis; Massachusetts–Boston; Michigan–Lansing; Minnesota–St. Paul; Mississippi–Jackson; Missouri–Jefferson City; Montana–Helena; Nebraska–Lincoln; Nevada–Carson City; New Hampshire–Concord; New Jersey–Trenton; New Mexico–Santa Fe; New York–Albany; North Carolina–Raleigh; North Dakota–Bismarck; Ohio–Columbus; Oklahoma–Oklahoma City; Oregon–Salem; Pennsylvania–Harrisburg; Rhode Island–Providence; South Carolina–Columbia; South Dakota–Pierre; Tennessee–Nashville; Texas–Austin; Utah–Salt Lake City; Vermont–Montpelier; Virginia–Richmond; Washington–Olympia; West Virginia–Charleston; Wisconsin–Madison; Wyoming–Cheyenne

Holiday Scramble (page 73)

Valentine's Day; Christmas; St. Patrick's Day; Passover; Thanksgiving Day; Fourth of July; Good Friday; April Fools' Day; Labor Day; Memorial Day

Christmas Quiz (page 103)

(1) False. Jesus' birth is recorded in the books of Matthew and Luke. (2) False. They traveled to Bethlehem for Jesus' birth. They lived in Nazareth later. (3) True (see Matthew 1:20-21). (4) False. She put cloths in the manger, not hay (see Luke 2:7). (5) True (see Luke 1:31). (6) False. They came later (see Matthew 2:1-11). By the way, we really don't know how many Magi came from the East. (7) True. He is also the light of the world, conceived by the Holy Spirit around the time of the Jewish Festival of the Lights.

FOR MORE INFORMATION

Contact Author/Speaker
Lynne Thompson at:

SoccerMomBook.com
Lynne@LynneThompson.net

Dedicated to encouraging women with a
van load of God's truth and
a sport bottle filled with laughter.